THE TRUEWEALTH
FAMILY LEGACY BLUEPRINT

THE COMPLETE ESTATE PLAN
TO PROTECT YOUR FAMILY
AND LEAVE A LEGACY
OF WEALTH AND WISDOM

CATHERINE HAMMOND, Esq.

The TrueWealth Family Legacy Blueprint:

The Complete Estate Plan to Protect Your Family and Leave a Legacy of Wealth and Wisdom

Disclaimer: The author is an attorney licensed only in Colorado. Any information provided here is not legal advice for you or your family, but general legal information. Recommendations for you and your family can't be given without a conversation about your situation, assets, goals, and concerns. Please consult with an experienced attorney in your state who focuses only on estate planning. The tools and strategies detailed in this book are not guaranteed to produce any specific results. The author is not a licensed therapist. If you need support personally or with your relationships, please seek guidance from a licensed professional. To maintain client confidentiality, amalgams of client stories were created using AI.

Design and cover art by Dino Marino, www.dinomarinodesign.com

Paperback ISBN: 979-8-9860105-0-2

eBook ISBN: 979-8-9860105-1-9

"*The TrueWealth Family Legacy Blueprint* is a timely wake-up call for families and advisors who are beginning to sense that something vital is missing in traditional estate planning. With clarity and compassion, Catherine Hammond reveals how *TrueWealth*—the integration of financial and human capital—can break cycles of silence, distance, and pain. This book is an invitation to create *Generational Wholeness* by sharing stories, values, and intentional love before it's too late."

~ John A. Warnick, Founder, Purposeful Planning Institute | Attorney | Author of The Gift of You

"As a former practicing attorney and current CEO of Trustee Services Group, I've had the honor of overseeing the estate plans of countless families, and the privilege of intimately interacting with the generations whom they wish to benefit. Catherine Hammond's The TrueWealth Family Legacy Blueprint addresses exactly what we see is sorely missing to best ensure a generationally successful wealth transfer: the values, stories, and guidance that could help heirs responsibly receive and steward their inheritance by understanding how their gift was intended to be a personal and thoughtful investment in their well-being as opposed to just an administratively cold transfer of assets. Her systematic approach to cultivating and transferring the much-needed personal aspects, alongside the legal structure and financial elements, aligns perfectly with our work as Trustee and Estate Fiduciary. This book transforms estate planning from a technical exercise into true family legacy building. We'll be recommending this important resource to advisors and the families we have the privilege of serving so their estate plan can become what most wealth holders desire . . . a thoughtful investment in the betterment of their loved ones."

~ Steve Marken, JD | Founder & CEO, Trustee Services Group

"Catherine is visionary and inspiring, her message will transform families for generations."

~ Chip Conley, Founder Modern Elder Academy | NYT Bestselling Author

"I wish this book had been published during my grandparents' lifetime. My family lost its wealth in the second generation and fractured family relationships in the process. If this book had been available to my grandparents, it could very well have changed the trajectory of my family's financial resources and family relationships. And that's not hyperbole.

Catherine Hammond is that rare trust and estates attorney who recognizes that "intergenerational wholeness" (a term she coined, which I love), requires you to be as purposeful in passing on to future generations who you are, as you are in passing on to them what you own. Yet, estate planning is generally focused almost exclusively on what you own. Catherine has gone beyond recognizing that conventional planning is lacking and taken creative action to help fill the void with her TrueWealth Family Legacy℠ Framework.

In *The TrueWealth Family Legacy Blueprint*, she lays out the framework and guides you through it step-by-step. Catherine shows you how to share with your family the stories, wisdom and love that define who you are and offer them meaning beyond money. She's included practical tools, insightful reflection questions and an array of options to help you draw out, articulate and share these priceless gifts that only you can give your family. The emotionally rewarding journey and deeper family connections will be an invaluable gift to yourself, as well."

~Thomasina Williams, JD | Strategic Thought Partner, Coach & Consultant to Enterprising Families

"Catherine Hammond has taken the wisdom of those of us who believe in "purposeful estate planning" and taken BIG steps towards helping clients actually IMPLEMENT the keys to success. Many of us know that the most successful wealth transfers happen when clients pass on their values, stories, and wisdom alongside their financial assets. Her TrueWealth approach helps create 'living documents'—estate plans that breathe with meaning and purpose rather than sterile legal language. For families or advisors who have completed their estate planning documents but feel that "something is missing," Catherine's TrueWealth approach and book is essential reading for creating and passing on their life's and heart's work."

~ Curtis Kaiser, JD, MBA | Founder, Kaiser Law Group

"As a financial advisor and fiduciary with over 30 years of experience directly advising clients, I have observed the positive and negative side of wealth and its potential impact on families. It has the ability to create and destroy. I am a firm believer in planning when it comes to managing and transferring wealth. This is even more critical in an estate setting. Catherine Hammond's book, *The TrueWealth Family Legacy Blueprint*, is a brilliant tool to aid families struggling with the responsibility that comes along with wealth. It has a unique approach encompassing more than transferring the wealth itself: human capital (values) is an integral part of the process in addition to financial capital. Finally, this book presents its information in an intuitive and illustrative fashion with great examples and fun stories.."

~ Brad Harvey, JD, CFP | President & CEO,
Harvey Investment Management, Inc.

"As a financial advisor, I've gotten to know many estate planning attorneys over the years. However, I've never met one like Catherine Hammond who puts as much thought into what really matters – your true legacy, or as she puts it, your TrueWealth. Her process leads with the human aspect – the legacy you want to leave and the lessons you want to impart to your loved ones, rather than just creating legal paperwork. Guess which part is going to be the most impactful to your loved ones? This book shows you how the combination of your financial capital with your human capital – your wisdom, life stories, lessons and love – is what truly helps your family for generations, and perhaps even changes the trajectory of your family story. This book will change the way you view the estate planning process!"

~ Paul Franco, MBA, CFP |
Founder, Life Well Lived Financial Group

"I coach exceptional leaders who've achieved financial success but still struggle with feeling 'enough', and Catherine Hammond's *The TrueWealth Family Legacy Blueprint* addresses the missing piece I see in so many of their lives. Her concept of intergenerational wholeness resonates deeply with my work because it shows how our deepest wounds and greatest wisdom can become gifts rather than burdens for future generations. This book transforms the very definition of wealth from external metrics to internal truth. For any leader who wants to pass on more than money—who wants to be remembered for who they were, not just what they accumulated—this book is essential reading."

~ Mandy Lehto,
Executive Coach and host of Enough, the Podcast

"Catherine is inspiring in how she redefines estate planning. Her methodology blends wealth, wisdom, legacy, and the deeper meaning of money to create lasting family harmony and purpose."

~ Kate Duffy, Financial Advisor |
Certified Financial Behavior Specialist

"Catherine Hammond's work doesn't just change how you think about legacy—it transforms how you live and love today. When I participated in one of Catherine's programs I felt compelled to write a letter to my 12-year-old daughter 'in case something happened to me.' When I told her what I'd done, her response stopped me in my tracks: 'I might die before you, Dad. I'd like to do that for you as well, so you've got something to read.' That moment brought tears to my eyes and showed me the profound impact this work has on entire families, not just the person going through the process. But what surprised me most was that the transformation wasn't just in the letter I wrote—it was in how this work freed me to express love without reservation in my daily life. After experiencing Catherine's approach, I now see differently what legacy truly means and feel inspired to create deeper connections with my family every day. *The TrueWealth Family Legacy Blueprint* is desperately needed because families everywhere are missing the wisdom, stories, and love that create intergenerational wholeness. This moving book shows us how to break through the barriers that keep us from sharing what matters most while we're still here to share it. If you have people you love, don't wait—this work will change not just your legacy, but your life."

~ Chris Joseph, PhD. | Transformational Coach,
Trusted Advisor & Mindfulness Practitioner

"I've spent the last 13 years discussing money and wealth with families, first as a financial advisor and then as a financial coach. What Catherine Hammond addresses in *The TrueWealth Family Legacy Blueprint* is the missing piece that ALL families need in their financial conversations! Most money problems aren't really about money at all -- they are about values, communication, and unresolved family money patterns. This book gives families profound insights and practical tools to change future generations and create more meaning and purpose through their money. I love how this book transforms the concept of intergenerational wealth beyond just a financial figure - but rather into sharing how *everyone*, regardless of their financial standing, can leave a meaningful legacy for future generations!"

~ Jordan Pendleton, Money Relationship Coach | Former Financial Advisor

"At 84, I've come to realize that the tangibles I've accumulated and shared over my lifetime, while not without value, do not constitute the most important legacy I leave my sons and grandchildren. Dreams deferred, dreams derailed, and dreams delightedly discovered to have been actualized over these decades—such are at the heart of my true legacy. Catherine Hammond's *The TrueWealth Family Legacy Blueprint* offers families like mine a unique process and opportunity to share those hopes and values by which we define ourselves. What moves me most about this work is how it allows us to share who we are as complete persons, not simply in our 'father' or 'grandfather' roles. I hope and pray that through Catherine's approach, these life perspectives can become central anchors for the life horizons of our surviving family members, insofar as they might choose for themselves. This book provides the framework for passing on what truly matters most."

~ Joseph Forgue, Spiritual Director

To my beloved daughters, Kayla and Marisa,

and my precious grandchildren

Sequoia, Esmé, Rosela, and Tino

You have taught me more about living fully, bravely, and beautifully than you could ever know.

You are everything that our ancestors hoped and

dreamed for the future; know that they are with you.

With giant hugs and all my love,

Mama/Mimi

TABLE OF CONTENTS

INTRODUCTION

THE GIFT THAT CHANGES EVERYTHING

Most people believe they've taken great care of their families for the long run once they complete their estate plan. You may know how this feels; you sign a Will or Trust, designate beneficiaries for your accounts, set up tax-saving strategies, and check "estate and legacy planning" off your list. It feels responsible, comprehensive, and loving. You heave a sigh of relief and finally have peace of mind about protecting your loved ones when you're no longer here.

But what if I told you that there's still something missing, something beyond the legal papers and financial arrangements? I believe traditional estate planning only addresses half of what your loved ones truly need from you, and it's not the most important half.

After helping nearly 5,000 families as an estate planning attorney, I've seen a striking pattern emerge: The families who truly thrive after a loved one's passing aren't usually those who received the largest financial inheritance or the most tax-efficient estate plan. They're the ones who received something far more precious — what I call your "TrueWealth."

TrueWealth is the combination of your financial capital (the money and assets you leave behind) *and* your human capital (your wisdom, life stories, and love). It's everything that makes you uniquely you — the experiences that shaped you, the lessons you've learned, and the love you hold for those who matter most.

This book exists for two deeply important reasons:

First, to transform how you think about your wealth and legacy, helping you give your loved ones what they truly need most from you.

Second, to provide you with practical tools and strategies that will create deeper connections in your family while building your legacy, one that ensures you pass what's most important to you and will benefit your family for generations to come — regardless of where your family relationships stand today.

As we journey through these pages together, I promise to be honest with you about what I've learned over the last several decades working closely with families as loved ones become disabled or pass away. My experience has taught me that truly helping people requires truth, practical solutions, and compassion. You'll find all three here.

This book is for you if you want to be more than just the parent who raised children to adulthood or the aunt who had fun with your nieces and nephews when you spent time with them. It's for you if you want your wisdom, life stories, and love (alongside any financial inheritance) to continue guiding and nourishing your family long after you're gone.

I want to help you create a legacy that matters—one that continues to support and guide your loved ones even after you're gone—and a life that feels even more purposeful, connected, and meaningful every day that you're here. To do that, here's how I've structured this book:

First, we'll take an honest look at your current estate and legacy plan to discover what might be missing. Through several self-assessments, you'll uncover gaps between what you hope to leave behind and what you're actually on track to provide. These assessments are based on patterns I've observed across thousands of families—both those who thrived after a loved one's passing and those who struggled despite significant financial inheritance.

Next, I'll show you why integrating your human capital with your financial capital creates a truly meaningful legacy. You'll discover that many family difficulties after a loved one's passing stem from focusing solely on financial assets while neglecting the non-financial elements.

We'll examine the four major challenges that traditional estate planning fails to address, understand why people procrastinate on this vital work, and then break through those barriers to help you get started now.

Then, I'll share with you the complete TrueWealth Family Legacy℠ System, from top to bottom. This is the same methodology I use with clients who want to leave a lasting legacy that truly helps their loved ones thrive for generations. I'm excited to share it with you here in detail.

As part of that, we'll spend significant time focusing on how to discover, cultivate, and gift your wisdom, your life stories, and your love in lasting ways. I'll show you how to identify the experiences that shaped you, how to extract the wisdom from those experiences, and even how to preserve your legacy in ways that future generations will actually engage with.

The goal is for you to begin implementing at least one aspect of this planning by the time you finish reading this book—and to start experiencing the benefits in your own life immediately.

Finally, we'll explore practical implementation strategies tailored to your unique family situation. I'll show you how to create your personalized TrueWealth Family Legacy℠ Road Map and integrate your non-financial legacy with your existing financial and legal arrangements.

That might sound like a lot, but the heart of this book boils down to three essential truths:

Truth #1: For thousands of years, wisdom and stories have been humanity's most valuable inheritance, creating resilience that carries families through economic, social, and personal challenges.

Truth #2: The more you cultivate and share your human capital alongside your financial capital, the more meaningful impact you'll have on future generations — and the richer your own life becomes now.

Truth #3: The most effective way to discover, cultivate, and gift what matters most is through the TrueWealth Family Legacy℠ System you'll find in this very book.

This isn't just about what happens after you're gone. The process of cultivating your human capital will transform your life for every day that you're still here. People who complete this journey often tell me they feel more alive than they have in years. They discover a deeper sense of meaning and purpose. Their relationships improve. The approach you're about to discover has profoundly transformed the lives of my clients and their families, with benefits that extend far beyond financial security. It's especially powerful for those who want to be remembered not just for what they achieved, but for how they loved and what they stood for.

If you take nothing else from this book, remember this: the most important parts of you don't have to die when you do.

It is my deepest hope that you learn more than just how to implement the system I've created. Throughout these pages, I've woven in insights and lessons from three decades of helping families navigate the emotional terrain of estate and legacy planning. Yes, this is a book about estate planning, but it's really a book about creating intergenerational wholeness and ensuring your loved ones have what they truly need most from you.

I sincerely believe that families can and should be sources of strength, identity, and love across generations. I believe it will be thoughtful individuals like you who make that happen through intentional legacy planning that goes beyond money—those who aim to be healing presences in their family lines.

It's a privilege to share what I've learned with you. I hope it inspires and equips you to cultivate these other facets of your wealth, so you can provide your loved ones with the guidance and love they'll need long after you're gone.

And a special note to those who don't have "perfect" families: you are not alone. In fact, those "perfect" families you think you see throughout your community? They have their own struggles and challenges too. More than 27% of Americans are estranged from at least one family member, and many more have relationships that don't match the idealized image we carry of what family "should" be.

I'm here to help real families — just like yours — whether your relationships are everything you've dreamed of, or whether you're longing for more connection with the people you love. This book is for those who want to be the kind of ancestors you wish you had, leaving clear guideposts for your descendants as they navigate life's challenges.

I've learned most of what I share here the hard way — through my own family trials and by walking hand-in-hand with hundreds of families through the disability and death of their loved ones. There are simple tools you can use to maximize connection and the power of family, no matter your starting place, and we'll explore them together in this book.

This book is full of stories from my life and those I know and have worked with. To preserve the confidentiality of my clients, names and/or details of their stories have been changed. Some of the stories are amalgams of multiple people to preserve anonymity.

As you read this book and learn about the methods I teach, you may want personalized guidance implementing these strategies, and I'd love to help. Please visit:

TrueWealthFamily.com

Helping people like you discover, cultivate, and gift your TrueWealth is exactly what my team and I do every day.

We're here to help.

With love and belief in the power of your legacy,

Catherine Hammond

PART 1

WHY TRUEWEALTH MATTERS MORE THAN MONEY

CHAPTER 1

A NEW REALITY- BEYOND TRADITIONAL ESTATE PLANNING

FROM PERSONAL PAIN TO PROFESSIONAL PURPOSE: WHERE IT ALL BEGAN

My story with estate planning began when I was about 12 years old. One Saturday morning I walked into my mother's bathroom, where she stood brushing her once-vibrant red hair. As I walked in, she reached down to the counter and picked up a newspaper article she'd carefully cut out of the Denver Post. Her fingers trembled as she handed it to me and said, "I think I have this."

The only reason I'd come into her bathroom was to ask if I could walk over to my best friend's house, but at that moment, everything shifted.

"How do you pronounce this?" I asked, my eyes fixed on the strange word in the headline.

"It's *Alz-heim-er's*," she said softly.

My mom spent her life as a teacher, her mind a tapestry of knowledge and wit that educated and entertained everyone who knew her. Even now she was teaching me, though neither of us fully understood the journey we were beginning.

In the 1970s, hardly anyone had heard of Alzheimer's Disease. People talked about senility or losing your memory in old age, but Alzheimer's and dementia weren't part of our collective vocabulary yet.

With her quick mind and a curiosity that ran deep, finding an article about some obscure disease wasn't out of character for my loving mom. But the look in her eyes as she handed it to me – that mixture of fear and resignation – that was new. She wasn't just interested in this disease; she believed it was already taking over her brain.

At 12, I was sure I knew everything. I certainly knew better than my mom. And I was positive she didn't have this disease, she was just crazy.

I began to read the article while she stood there, the morning light highlighting her vulnerability in her bra and underwear. As I continued reading, I discovered this article was talking about memory loss *in old people*. I felt my frustration rise. Why was she making this up, saying that she had a disease that was clearly for people in their 80s or beyond? She was only in her 40s.

I rolled my eyes, an art I'd been perfecting at that age, and quietly put the article back down on her bathroom counter. The familiar ache of disappointment hit me right in my chest. Why was she always doing something weird and embarrassing? Why couldn't she just be like the other moms, baking cookies and fixing my hair, guiding me through this difficult season?

After years of her debilitating depression, my young mind and heart couldn't accept that I might be losing what little I'd had in the mother department. As I navigated the waters of puberty and the mean girls at school, what I longed for more than anything was for my mom to wrap her arms around me and tell me everything would be okay. I needed her to be my safe harbor, not another storm I had to weather.

But on that sunny Saturday morning, I swallowed my disappointment and settled for walking over to my best friend's house. There I could pretend, at least for a few hours, that everything in my world was just fine.

What I didn't know yet was that in handing me that article about Alzheimer's Disease my mom had just handed me a burden most people don't have to carry until the twilight of their lives. And I was about to discover that my life wouldn't follow the "normal" script I so desperately wanted.

WHEN EVERYTHING FELL APART: THE COLLEGE YEARS CRISIS

Fast forward to my junior year of college. The dorm room phone rang, piercing the comfortable bubble I'd created for myself thousands of miles from home. My mom's voice came through the line, thin and frightened, telling me she was losing her job as a special education teacher. They claimed she couldn't manage the paperwork anymore, but she insisted through tears that it wasn't true, that someone at school just "had it out for her."

The familiar mixture of love, guilt, and resentment churned in my stomach.

Within six months after my college graduation, over chips and chunky salsa at her favorite Mexican restaurant, she slid a paper across the table. It was her doctor's assessment. She no longer remembered how to draw a clock. And, according to him, she couldn't live by herself anymore. She officially had this disease called Alzheimer's.

The restaurant noise faded as I stared at the page. As I took in what I read, I could feel something breaking inside me, but my head was spinning too quickly to identify exactly what it was.

She was a single mom, and while my older brother lived in town, it turned out he wasn't interested in helping take care of her. My younger brother was away at college, wrestling with a surprisingly large but benign brain tumor. So, figuring out what to do next fell to me, the middle child, the girl who had spent her life trying to hold everything together.

THE LEGAL SYSTEM THAT FAILED US BOTH

The reality hit me like a physical blow when I discovered I couldn't just sell my mom's house to move her into a nursing home. Like so many of the clients I've now worked with in my legal practice, she didn't have the right paperwork in place. Her doctor gave me the name of a lawyer, and soon I was sitting across a polished conference table from her.

I was trying so hard to be an adult, to be strong, to be whatever my mother needed me to be with our roles fully reversed. But when the lawyer told me about the long, complicated, expensive legal process ahead, the tears I'd been holding back for what felt like my entire life finally broke free. They weren't delicate tears that trickled gracefully down my cheeks. They were messy, ugly sobs that shook my whole body and separated me from everything else in the room.

The alarm bells had been ringing for ten years, but we still weren't prepared. With the official diagnosis I couldn't ignore her dementia anymore. I took on the job of managing her life with a mixture of love, determination, and resentment so deep it physically hurt.

I was 22. All my friends were having fun and discovering who they wanted to be. But not me. I was in nursing homes and lawyers' offices, making life-or-death decisions no young person should have to make.

THE LONG GOODBYE: 20 YEARS OF LOSS

I put everything on hold to take care of my mom, visiting care communities until I found an assisted living that seemed right – warm staff, clean rooms, pictures on the walls that made it feel less institutional. I moved her in, crying silently as she held her favorite sweater to her chest and asked me, repeatedly, when we were going home.

Two days later, the first of many surprising calls came. My mom had been walking into other people's apartments naked, and I had to find her a new home in 24 hours. I hung up the phone and slid down the wall to the floor, hugging my knees to my chest. I wished I could just disappear.

I stayed up all night worrying, my mind racing with possibilities, none of them good. Then at 8 a.m., I kicked into achievement mode, the mode that had gotten me through so much already. After what felt like hundreds of phone calls, I finally found a group home that agreed to take her in.

As I dropped her off later that day, nearly two hours away from home, I felt like I was abandoning her. But what choice did I have? The guilt and grief settled into my bones.

She had a new home, but I still needed to sell her house. I spent my nights and weekends sorting through the physical evidence of her life: piles of magazines she'd meant to read, clothes she'd bought and never worn, collector's plates and stamps she'd been sure would be worth something someday. Each item I touched felt like a piece of her I was discarding, but for lack of anything else to do with the houseful of possessions I threw most of them in the trash. After more than a month, my heart raw, I finally gave up and called someone to clean out the rest and take it to the dump.

My mom spent 20 years in a nursing home, the last 11 of them in a vegetative state. I watched as she slowly disappeared, piece by piece, until all that was left was the shell of the woman who had once cut out newspaper articles and tried desperately to hold onto her children and remaining memories as they slipped through her fingers. She finally passed away in a mess of end-of-life decisions I was totally unprepared to make, standing alone at the edge of the abyss I'd been circling for most of life.

FINDING PURPOSE IN THE PAIN: A NEW KIND OF LEGAL PRACTICE

I share this story because life happens. And if we don't prepare well, it's our families who pay the price.

After a lifetime of making our children buckle their seatbelts and eat their vegetables, all it takes is *one sudden tragedy* to mess up our plans to take good care of our families when we exit this life. We know logically that tragedy could strike at any time, and most of us have a voice in the back of our minds worrying that something could happen to us until ... a colleague, friend, or family member gets a diagnosis or has an accident, and we think: what if that was me? What if something happens to me and I become a burden to my family?

What happened to my mom was tragic, but it's far from unique. We are—every one of us—like beautiful ice sculptures melting slowly, until we fade away completely. We know our trajectory; we know that life on earth is temporary.

Honestly, the legal system left me feeling like I'd been beaten up in a boxing match. Even with a lawyer, I had to provide endless information, sign dozens of documents, and request permission for every little thing I needed to do for my mom. My attorney had saved me with her nurturing care, and one day in her office, wrapping up the mess because my mom didn't have any legal documents in place, I decided to go to law school so I could help other people prepare better for their loved ones.

At least I could make something good out of the heartache I experienced. By getting legal documents in place before disability or death, I could help people pass their money and other assets to their loved ones in a smoother way than what I experienced. I graduated law school in 1993.

In 2005, frustrated with the failure of so many law firms to focus on clients rather than billable hours, I founded my own estate planning law firm. I was a single mom to two precious girls and struggling to pay my hefty student loans along with the mortgage, so it wasn't much of a "law firm" back then. It was my kitchen table. I met with new clients in the conference room of an executive suite, then rushed home to start drafting their documents in my kitchen before my daughters came home from school.

Within a few months I had enough clients to move into an office, and soon I hired a paralegal. The rapid growth of my firm confirmed the need for an estate and elder law practice with a talented team who truly love serving clients, and it's our team who enabled us to serve more than 5,000 families over the last 20 years. Clients love the people-centric approach to estate planning, built on what I'd learned from my mom's tragedy: it's best to keep things out of probate court, both if you're incapacitated and when you die. Most of my clients set up Revocable Living Trusts for this reason, to make things as easy as possible for their loved ones in the most difficult moments of life.

THE MISSING PIECE THAT CHANGES EVERYTHING

Over time I saw something surprising. Even clients who set up perfect estate plans still didn't adequately prepare their families for what would come after they passed away. And after watching good estate plans fail family after family, I realized that money isn't what their children need most.

It's certainly not what I needed.

Sure, I would have loved to inherit millions of dollars from my mom, but what I truly long for is more of *her*. Her wisdom, her life stories, and her love.

This realization led me to develop a new approach: helping people leave a legacy that truly helps families thrive.

Let me show you the difference this makes through the experiences of two families ...

IMAGINE TWO FAMILIES GATHERING AFTER THE LOSS OF BELOVED PARENTS.

Both sets of parents left behind carefully drafted legal documents and decent financial inheritances, about $4 million each, equally divided among their children.

Bob and Edna Wyatt had raised a loving family and set up their children's inheritance to make sure all their assets were passed along smoothly. The Wyatt siblings—Amy, Mark, and Susan—received their inheritance just as their parents had planned. The funds transferred efficiently through their well-designed living trust. The legal documents worked exactly as intended.

Yet within a year, their family was unrecognizable. Mark never spoke to Amy again after he got mad because his parents had chosen her as trustee. He spent most of his inheritance within two years. Susan, devastated by losing her parents, dropped out of graduate school and struggled to find her way. Amy, though successful in her medical career, felt she had failed her parents' wish for the family to remain close. She vowed never to have children of her own to avoid passing on these painful family patterns.

Their financial inheritance couldn't prevent, and in some ways even accelerated, the breakdown of what mattered most.

The Millers took a different approach. Like the Wyatts, they created solid legal documents. But they also recorded their life stories, wrote heartfelt letters to each child addressing their unique strengths and challenges, documented the meaning behind family heirlooms, and expressed their deepest wisdom, values, and dreams for future generations.

Today, several years after both parents passed away, the Miller siblings remain connected. They use their inheritance purposefully and continue to draw strength from the wisdom their parents left behind. When conflicts arise, they refer to the values their parents articulated. When facing major life decisions, they listen to recordings of their parents sharing wisdom from similar crossroads in their own lives. Family gatherings include sharing stories their parents preserved, keeping their presence alive for grandchildren and now great-grandchildren who never met them.

The difference wasn't in the amount of money these families left behind—it was in the human element. This human element—what I call your TrueWealth—carries the power to transform how your family navigates life after losing their loved ones. It's your hard-won wisdom, the life stories that make you and those who came before you unique, and the love you have for those you treasure most.

WHAT LIFE LOOKS LIKE WHEN YOU'VE PREPARED YOUR TRUEWEALTH

Let's look at what life is like for families who have received both financial capital and human capital from their parents and grandparents.

For the Martins, family movie night has taken on new meaning since their grandmother Eleanor's passing. Before starting the film, they play a short video message she recorded specifically for moments like these. Eleanor's face appears on screen, her eyes twinkling as she reminds them how much she treasured these gatherings. "Remember," she says, "the movie isn't what matters. It's sitting shoulder to shoulder, laughing together, arguing over the plot twists. That's where the magic happens." Her grandson Tyler, who was only five when she died, knows her voice, her mannerisms, and most importantly her wisdom.

When Lisa Patterson's daughter faced a difficult decision about whether to take a job across the country, she found herself rereading the letter her mother had written about her own choice to move away from family for career advancement. "I worried I was being selfish," Lisa had written, "but I realized that honoring your own path is itself a form of honoring your family. The gifts and talents you've been given need room to grow." That letter, part of a collection Lisa had created addressing major life milestones, provided exactly the wisdom her daughter needed in that moment, years after Lisa's passing.

James Wilson's sons gather annually to make decisions about the family foundation their father established. Before beginning, they reread the family values statement James created with them before his death. "Our wealth is a tool for creating opportunity, not a substitute for hard work," it reminds them. "We value education, compassion, and lifting others as we rise." This clarity of purpose has prevented countless disagreements over the years and kept the family aligned in their philanthropic efforts. James had fulfilled his desire to be a legacy builder who left both financial resources and moral guidance for future generations.

These families aren't perfect. They face conflicts, make mistakes, and experience all the usual complexities of family life. What's different is how they navigate these challenges with the continued guidance of loved ones who prepared and shared their non-financial legacies in addition to their money.

STORIES OF TRANSFORMATION

The impact of cultivating and leaving your TrueWealth isn't limited to what happens after someone passes away. The very process of cultivating and sharing your wisdom, life story, and love transforms relationships in the present.

Consider Gene, my 70-something year old neighbor. Last year I ran into him when I was out for my morning walk. Another neighbor had recently passed away, so Gene was thinking about his mortality.

"I need to update my Will, but I don't know what to do. I don't want to leave everything to my daughter, she's not that motivated to work anyway. I'm afraid she'd just blow the money," he says.

"Have you thought about leaving a letter with your Will that says how much you love her?" I ask.

"No, that's a good idea, but I don't know how to do that. I don't really know how to express my emotions." So I offer him two simple questions: "what are a few specific things you love about her or you're proud of?" and "what are your hopes and dreams for her future?" And I invite him to write down the answers as a starting place. With tears in his eyes, this neighbor I barely knew, the one who didn't know how to express his emotions, gave me a big hug and said thank you.

A couple months later I'm on my morning walk again and Gene comes running up to me. "Catherine, I'm so glad to see you! You're not going to believe what's happened to my relationship with my daughter. Everything has changed!"

Gene hasn't even finished writing the letter, but when he stops to think about his relationship with his daughter, he realizes some things that change his behavior. He starts calling and texting her more often. And when he adjusts his behavior, she responds differently. She texts and calls more often and even stops by to see him. They're hugging more. They both start reaching towards each other and have a relationship today that almost didn't happen.

Then there's Elena, who had inherited her mother's jewelry collection but rarely wore any pieces because they felt like "just things" to her. When she began documenting the stories behind family heirlooms as part of her TrueWealth planning, she discovered that the simple pearl necklace she'd dismissed had been given to her mother by her grandfather and had come at a great sacrifice. He'd chosen to sell his prized fishing boat to be able to give her that gift when she got married.

"Now when I wear those pearls, I feel connected to a story of sacrifice and love spanning three generations," Elena explained. "What was once just a necklace in a drawer has become one of my most treasured possessions."

Without these stories, countless family treasures end up in estate sales or landfills, their significance lost forever. With these stories preserved, even the simplest objects become vessels of family identity and connection.

WHAT TO EXPECT WHEN YOU IMPLEMENT TRUEWEALTH PLANNING

As you begin implementing the TrueWealth blueprint I'll share in this book, you can expect both immediate and long-term benefits.

Many people experience the surprising and immediate benefit that Gene did: a deepening of current relationships. The process of reflecting on your values, clarifying what matters most, and beginning to share your wisdom often leads to more authentic connections with loved ones. Conversations move beyond surface topics to what truly matters.

Misunderstandings that have festered for years often heal when brought into the light of intentional communication.

"I thought this was something I was doing for my kids after I'm gone," one client told me. "I had no idea how much it would transform our relationship while I'm still here. I didn't even realize our relationship could get better."

For yourself, the process brings unexpected gifts. Many people report a deeper sense of meaning and purpose as they recognize the value of their life experience. There's also a profound satisfaction in knowing you've done everything possible to help your loved ones thrive, not just financially, but emotionally and spiritually as well.

"I feel more alive than I have in years," another client shared. "Looking back at my life's journey, seeing the patterns, extracting the wisdom — it's made me appreciate how much I've learned and how much I still have to offer."

Over time, the impact extends far beyond what you might imagine. Your wisdom becomes a resource your children and grandchildren draw upon throughout their lives. Your stories provide a sense of belonging and identity that research shows is crucial for psychological wellbeing. Your love, tangibly expressed, continues to nurture and support long after you're gone. You become someone who is planting trees whose shade your descendants will sit under, investing in a future that will benefit those you love, for generations.

While your financial legacy may indeed provide important opportunities and security, it's the addition of your human capital that will truly help your loved ones navigate life's challenges and find fulfillment.

This book will guide you through the process of cultivating and sharing the other pieces of your TrueWealth: your wisdom, life story, and love. You'll discover practical tools for capturing what matters most and effectively passing it to future generations. Along the way, you'll gain clarity about your own values and purpose, potentially transforming not just your legacy but the life you're living right now.

The wisdom and stories you cultivate for the coming generations are not meant to replace the wisdom they will inevitably gain through living their own lives, but to enhance it. To offer a foundation upon which they can build. It's not meant to be commands from the grave, but an offering of loving guidance based on your hard-won insights.

The traditional approach to estate planning focuses almost exclusively on financial assets and legal documents. I'm inviting you to a new reality, one where what you leave behind includes not just what you owned but the most important parts of who you are. This approach speaks directly to those who want to be remembered not just for what they achieved, but for how they loved and what they stood for.

CHAPTER 1 TAKEAWAYS

- **Two Paths, Different Outcomes:** Traditional estate planning (focused solely on financial assets) often leads to family breakdown, while TrueWealth planning (combining financial and human capital) strengthens family bonds across generations.
- **Human Capital Matters Most:** Your wisdom, life stories, and love—your human capital—are more important to your loved ones than the financial assets you leave behind.
- **Transformation Begins Now:** Implementing TrueWealth principles brings immediate benefits to your current relationships while creating lasting impact for future generations.
- **Legacy Is More Than Money:** Even perfect legal documents cannot prevent family discord or future challenges for your descendants. What truly helps your family thrive is the wisdom and love you intentionally cultivate and share.
- **Stories Become Lifelines:** When you share your wisdom and experiences, they become resources your loved ones can draw upon long after you're gone, helping them navigate their own challenges with the benefit of your perspective.

REFLECTION ACTIVITY: YOUR LEGACY LANTERN

In this chapter I shared the story of Eleanor, who left a video for her family to watch when they gathered for movie nights. She may have had a few values or bits of wisdom in mind. She wanted to remind her family to make time for each other, to cherish the limited time they have together, and to savor the stories that make us human. What would your version of this video message to your family say?

Take 10-15 minutes to reflect on this question:

If you could leave behind one "lantern" to light the way for your loved ones after you're gone, what wisdom would it contain?

In your journal or on a separate sheet of paper:

1. Identify a challenge you've overcome that taught you something valuable about life.
2. Extract the wisdom from that experience. What did you learn that could help your loved ones navigate similar challenges?
3. Consider how this wisdom might serve as a guiding light for future generations of your family.
4. Write a brief message (2-3 sentences) capturing this wisdom as if you were speaking directly to someone you love who will read it years from now.

This simple exercise begins the process of identifying the elements of your human capital that matter most. As you continue through this book, you'll discover many more ways to cultivate and share your TrueWealth, but this first "lantern" represents an important first step in becoming the wisdom keeper and valuable ancestor you aspire to be.

CHAPTER 2

WHO THIS BOOK (AND MESSAGE) IS FOR

FINDING PURPOSE IN PREPARATION: THE JOURNEY TO TRUEWEALTH

The two stories I'm about to share reveal a common dilemma faced by loving families. While their circumstances differ, both illustrate why traditional estate planning often leaves us feeling that something essential is missing from our legacy.

David and Sarah's Story: Before Their TrueWealth Work

David and Sarah Reynolds had built an ideal family life over their 40 years of marriage. Their adult children, Michael (38) and Emma (35), remained unusually close, with Sunday dinners, active group texts, and family vacations continuing even as the family expanded with spouses and grandchildren.

Through decades of hard work, David's engineering firm and Sarah's accounting practice had built an $8 million estate that would provide substantial inheritance for their descendants.

As they entered their mid-sixties, two concerns began to shadow their contentment. The first surfaced after their youngest grandchild's birthday celebration.

"Did you notice how Emma kept taking pictures of everything today?" Sarah asked. "Not just the birthday moments, but all of us just sitting around talking."

"She told me she's been recording our family stories," David replied. "Said she doesn't want to forget a single one."

"They're preparing themselves," Sarah said quietly. "For when we're gone."

The realization hit them hard. Their family had created a beautiful interdependence: David saying the blessing at dinner, Sarah orchestrating holidays, both serving as confidants through life's challenges. What would happen without this emotional foundation?

Their second concern emerged as they discussed their estate.

"I worry about what all this money will mean for the grandkids," David said. "Whether they'll value work the way we do. Michael and Emma saw us build our businesses from nothing—the early mornings, the risks we took. But will Lily and Jacob understand that when they're handed substantial trusts without witnessing the work behind it?"

These twin concerns, that their children would be emotionally adrift without them, and that future generations might lose their family's values, weighed heavily.

"We've done all the practical stuff," David said. "The will, the trust, the advance directives. But none of that addresses either concern."

There was also wisdom they hadn't shared. David's battle with depression in his forties and Sarah nearly leaving the marriage during that crisis had shaped their approach to life, but they'd never disclosed these insights.

"I want our grandchildren to have more than just vague stories about us," Sarah told David. "I want them to feel connected to something bigger, to understand where they come from."

David nodded. "Remember that article about how children with a strong sense of family history tend to be more resilient?"

They worried that without intentional effort, their descendants would miss the anchor of identity that comes from understanding their family's journey and values. Who would tell the little ones about Great-Grandpa's immigration story or how their grandmother overcame childhood illness?

Sarah and David aren't the only ones who felt like passing money left something missing in their family.

A Different Perspective: Janet's Story Before Her TrueWealth Work

From the outside, Janet's life appeared perfect: a successful attorney in her early sixties with a thriving practice she built from the ground up, a beautiful home in a prestigious neighborhood, and adult children with promising careers of their own. Her estate planning documents were impeccable, after all she'd drafted countless wills and trusts for her clients over the years.

Yet when Janet closed her office door at night, a nagging sense of incompleteness followed her home. Despite decades of advising others on protecting their assets, she felt strangely unprepared for her own inevitable passing. Her legal documents were flawless, but something essential was missing.

Janet's relationship with her children was cordial but distant. They gathered for holiday dinners where conversations remained safely on the surface—work achievements, vacation plans, the grandchildren's latest milestones. When she tried to share stories from her own childhood or wisdom gained through difficult life experiences, her children seemed politely disinterested, checking their watches or steering the conversation back to practical matters.

"They'll appreciate my financial legacy someday," Janet told herself, pushing away the feeling that there was more she could—or should—be doing.

Janet lay awake some nights wondering: Would her children remember the values that guided her life decisions and use them to find their own guiding values? Would they learn from the mistakes she made along the way and understand the sacrifices she made to build her practice while raising them? Would they know how deeply she loved them, beyond the inheritance she'd leave behind? Most of all: Would they maintain connections with each other after she was gone?

WHO BENEFITS MOST FROM THE TRUEWEALTH APPROACH

David, Sarah, and Janet were facing what many loving parents eventually confront: preparing their children for a world without them requires more than excellent financial and legal planning. It demands preserving the nonmaterial aspects of inheritance—the wisdom, stories, values, and love that truly constitute a family's wealth.

This book is written for people who recognize that traditional estate planning—even when executed perfectly—addresses only a fraction of what truly matters when it comes to your legacy. It's for those who understand intuitively that while money and assets are important, they aren't what your loved ones will value most after you're gone.

You may be:

- A successful professional who has created financial security but worries about the impact of wealth on your children's motivation and values
- A grandparent concerned that family stories and traditions will fade away with your generation
- Someone who has experienced firsthand the devastation of family conflict after a parent's passing and is determined not to leave that legacy for your own children

- A person who has lost parents or grandparents and feels the absence of their wisdom and stories in your own life
- Someone facing a health challenge that has brought mortality into sharper focus, prompting deeper questions about what you'll leave behind
- A treasured aunt, uncle, other relative, or friend who cares deeply about the wellbeing of someone in a younger generation and knows that your wisdom, stories, and love will help create a solid foundation for your loved one(s)
- A person whose family relationships are currently strained, and you're seeking ways to heal disconnections or unhealthy patterns before it's too late; you want to be a healing presence in your family line
- Someone who has created an excellent financial estate plan but senses there's more to legacy than just money and legal documents

What unites all these people is a desire to create a legacy that encompasses not just what they own, but who they are, their wisdom, stories, values, and love.

My friend Luisa is a perfect example of how anyone can create a meaningful legacy. She doesn't have children of her own but takes an active role with her sister's kids. When her 7-year-old niece said she wanted to write a book when she grew up, Luisa said, "You don't have to wait until then, sweetie, you can do anything you want right now." Together they spent the next 6 months writing a children's book inspiring other kids to follow their dreams. Thanks to Luisa, her niece already knows she can do anything she wants.1 Whether you're a parent, grandparent, aunt, uncle, or treasured friend, you have the power to transform lives through your TrueWealth.

THE TRANSFORMATION: FROM TRADITIONAL ESTATE PLANNING TO TRUEWEALTH FAMILY LEGACY PLANNING

David and Sarah's Transformation

A year after beginning their TrueWealth journey, David and Sarah's family had transformed in ways they never expected.

Their Sunday dinners evolved from simple family gatherings into meaningful opportunities for connection. David began sharing stories about his depression in his forties, including how Sarah had stood by him despite considering leaving. These vulnerable disclosures sparked similar openness from Michael and Emma, who shared struggles they'd previously kept private.

"I always thought I needed to appear strong for our kids," David told Sarah one evening. "But sharing my struggles has somehow made them feel safer sharing theirs."

The process of documenting their values and wisdom wasn't just about what they would leave behind—it enriched their present relationships. When Emma faced a challenging career decision, rather than just offering advice, Sarah shared her own story of nearly abandoning her accounting practice during its difficult early years. This created a new dimension to their mother-daughter relationship.

Using the TrueWealth framework, their careful estate planning documents now existed alongside:

- Individual letters to each family member highlighting their unique gifts and the wisdom David and Sarah believed they might need at different life stages
- A collection of recorded conversations about family history, including Great-Grandpa's immigration story and Sarah's childhood illness

- A family mission statement developed collaboratively during a weekend retreat
- A digital archive of family photos and videos with recorded stories explaining their significance
- A catalog documenting meaningful heirlooms and the stories behind them
- A Book of Wisdom holding tidbits and lessons learned over their lifetimes

Most significantly, their grandchildren now had regular "wisdom sessions" where they asked questions about family history and values. Eight-year-old Jacob surprised everyone by asking David, "Grandpa, what's the hardest thing you ever had to do?" The conversation that followed created a connection neither had expected.

David and Sarah still worry about leaving their family someday, but the anxiety has been replaced with the peace of knowing they are actively passing on what matters most. Their TrueWealth journey hasn't just prepared their family for a future without them, it has deepened their current relationships in ways that make every day more meaningful.

Janet's Transformation

Let's return to Janet, just one year after implementing the TrueWealth approach you'll learn in this book.

The most immediate change? Her relationships with her children deepened significantly. What began as an intentional effort to document her life stories and wisdom evolved into healing conversations that addressed long-standing family patterns. Her adult children, initially skeptical about "mom's legacy project," gradually became engaged participants, asking questions about family history they'd never thought to ask before.

Janet discovered that the process of cultivating her TrueWealth wasn't just about what she would leave behind, it was transforming her life in the present. The reflection required to identify her most important values and life lessons brought new clarity to her daily decisions. She found herself spending less time at the office and more time on relationships and experiences aligned with what truly mattered to her.

When Janet's son faced a career crisis, instead of offering only financial support (her previous default), she shared the story of her own professional setback in her thirties, something she'd never discussed with her children before. That vulnerability created space for a connection deeper than they'd ever experienced. Her son later told her that knowing she had faced similar challenges gave him the courage to persevere.

Janet still had her impeccable legal documents. But now they were complemented by the gifts she had chosen for her loved ones:

- A series of letters to each child addressing their unique strengths, challenges, and the specific wisdom she believed they might need at different life stages
- An audio recording of family stories, including those passed down from her own parents and grandparents
- A documented "family legacy statement" that articulates the principles that guided her and her deepest hopes and dreams for future generations
- A catalog of meaningful family heirlooms with the stories and significance behind each one
- Video messages to be shared at specific future family milestones, including some she won't live to see

Most importantly, Janet had initiated healing conversations that had already strengthened family bonds. When her time comes, her children won't just inherit her assets, they'll inherit her wisdom, her stories, and tangible expressions of her love that will continue to nurture them throughout their lives.

The peace this brought Janet was immeasurable. She still lay awake sometimes, but now it was often to reflect on the meaningful conversations she was having with her children and to plan what stories she wanted to share next.

THIS SOUNDS GREAT, BUT ...

You might be thinking: "This sounds wonderful, but my situation is different."

Perhaps you're concerned that:

- You don't have a story worth telling
- You don't have a significant financial estate to leave behind
- You're not a gifted writer or storyteller
- Your family relationships are too complicated or damaged
- You're too young to be thinking about legacy planning
- You're already older and feel it's too late to start
- My kids are smart; they'll work it out like I had to!

Let me address these concerns directly:

"I don't have a story worth telling."

This concern is among the most common, and it's simply not true. You don't need to have climbed Mount Everest or built a Fortune 500 company for your story to matter profoundly to those you love. The seemingly ordinary moments of your life: your struggles, your triumphs, your daily choices; these are precisely what your descendants will treasure most, because these elements reveal the authentic you.

In fact, it's often the unvarnished, "ordinary" stories that provide the most meaningful connections across generations. Think about your own ancestors and the little details you treasure or wish you knew about their lives. Your descendants will feel the same way about you.

"I don't have much money to leave my loved ones."

The TrueWealth approach is just as important if your financial legacy is modest. Research shows that what adult children treasure most from their parents isn't money, but their wisdom, life stories, and love.

The financial services company Allianz conducted a study on legacy planning that yielded a surprising insight: when asked what they most hoped to receive from their parents' estate, the vast majority of baby boomers didn't list money or property first. Instead, 77% said that personal possessions with emotional significance and family stories were most important to them. In fact, they said that the non-financial legacy is ten times more important than the money and financial assets. By focusing on your human capital, you're giving your loved ones what they truly need most, regardless of your financial situation.

"I'm not a good writer or storyteller."

The TrueWealth framework offers multiple approaches to capturing and sharing your wisdom and stories, many of which don't require writing skills. Whether through recorded conversations, simple lists of life lessons, or guided exercises, you'll find methods that work for your unique abilities and preferences.

"My family relationships are complicated or damaged."

Complex or strained family relationships make this work more important, not less. The TrueWealth approach includes specific strategies for addressing family wounds and creating healing opportunities. While you cannot control how others respond, you can take steps toward reconciliation and clarity that might otherwise never happen. These steps will improve your life, create an opportunity to heal distant or estranged relationships, and provide a record of your wisdom, life stories, and love that will be available when they are ready. And they will be, eventually. The arc of the human heart bends towards healing, forgiveness, and reconciliation.

"I'm too young to be thinking about this."

Legacy planning isn't just for the elderly. Life is unpredictable, and a young parent has even more reason to leave their wisdom, stories, and love behind if your children end up without you at an early age. Additionally, cultivating your TrueWealth brings immediate benefits to your current relationships. Many people find that this process helps them live more intentionally and build stronger connections with family members across generations.

"I'm too old, it's too late to start."

As long as you're able to reflect on your life and communicate in some way, it's never too late to begin. Even small efforts to share your wisdom and love will be treasured by those you leave behind. The TrueWealth approach can be adapted for those with limited time or energy.

"My kids are smart; they'll work it out like I had to!"

There is an invisible danger to inherited money. Many of my clients didn't inherit wealth, they created it from humble beginnings. That's the difference between learning to drive in a beaten-up car and gradually developing your driving skills over successive faster cars versus being given the keys to a Ferrari on your 18th birthday and being told: "Go drive!" The TrueWealth system will help you pass the human capital that helps your loved ones "drive" a more complex vehicle than you may have inherited.

The truth is, if you care deeply about the long-term wellbeing of your loved ones and recognize that money alone can't secure it, this book is for you regardless of your age, financial status, or family circumstances.

WHY YOU MAY BE DISSATISFIED WITH TRADITIONAL ESTATE PLANNING

If you've already created a traditional estate plan, you probably heaved a sigh of relief knowing the legal aspects were handled. And then, at some point, maybe you discovered a nagging sense that something important remained unaddressed.

This feeling isn't unusual. Traditional estate planning focuses almost exclusively on what happens to your money and your stuff, not what happens to your people. It efficiently transfers assets but does nothing to pass on your wisdom, heal family wounds, or ensure that the values and lessons you've accumulated over a lifetime don't disappear when you do.

Consider these questions:

- Do your legal documents reflect not just what you want to happen to your assets, but why those wishes matter to you?
- Have you shared the life experiences and lessons that shaped your values with those who will inherit them?
- Will your loved ones understand the meaning behind the items you've chosen to leave them, and do they have the stories behind your possessions to carry that meaning forward into their own lives?
- Have you addressed potential sources of family conflict before they can erupt after you're gone?
- Have you created tangible expressions of your love that your family can turn to in happy and in difficult times?

If these questions highlight gaps in your current planning, you're not alone. The legal system simply wasn't designed to address these deeply human aspects of legacy.

That's precisely why I developed the TrueWealth Family Legacy[SM] System, to complement traditional estate planning with the elements that matter most for your family's long-term wellbeing.

Now, let's take a moment to assess where you currently stand in preparing your complete legacy. The following assessment will help you identify specific areas where implementing the TrueWealth approach could make the greatest difference for you and your loved ones.

TRUEWEALTH LEGACY ASSESSMENT

Rate yourself on a scale from 1-5 on how accurate each statement is—1 means "not accurate at all," and 5 means "completely accurate."

Once you've rated yourself for each statement, total up your scores and use the Answer Key to understand where you are on your TrueWealth journey.

LEGACY PREPARATION ASSESSMENT

Statement	Self Rating (1-5)
I have up-to-date legal documents (Will, Trust, Powers of Attorney, etc.) that clearly express my wishes.	________
I've had meaningful conversations with my loved ones about my values and what matters most to me.	________
My family understands the "why" behind my financial decisions and plans.	________
I've documented the stories behind important family heirlooms and keepsakes.	________
I've recorded or written down significant stories from my life that shaped who I am.	________
My loved ones know what I've learned from my greatest successes and most difficult challenges.	________
I've expressed my hopes and dreams for each of my loved ones in a way they can revisit in the future.	________
I've captured the insights I've gained through life experiences in a format my family can access.	________
I've preserved what I know of our family history and stories from previous generations, serving as a generational bridge between past and future.	________

Statement	**Self Rating (1-5)**
I feel confident my loved ones will maintain strong relationships with each other after I'm gone.	________
If I died tomorrow, my family would have access to messages of love and encouragement from me in the future, allowing me to be present even when I'm physically absent.	________
I've shared my deepest values with my loved ones in ways that will guide them after I'm gone.	________
I've created opportunities for healing in any strained family relationships, acting as a healing presence in my family line.	________
The non-financial parts of my legacy are as well-organized as my financial affairs.	________
I feel peace knowing I've done everything possible to help my loved ones thrive emotionally and spiritually after I'm gone.	________
My legal documents reflect my personal values and family dynamics, not just standard boilerplate language.	________
As a legacy builder, I've provided guidance about how I hope my financial assets might be used to benefit my loved ones.	________
I've preserved family traditions and their significance for future generations, serving as a memory guardian for our shared heritage.	________

Statement	Self Rating (1-5)
I can confidently say my loved ones feel truly known and valued by me.	________
I've reflected on and documented my own hard-earned wisdom and insights in a way that will help me become the kind of ancestor future generations will treasure.	________
TOTAL SCORE:	________

WHAT YOUR SCORE REVEALS ABOUT YOUR LEGACY

SCORE: 20-40

The Fundamentals Are Missing

You've recognized the importance of leaving a legacy, but you're just at the beginning of your journey. While you may have at least thought about creating legal documents, you haven't yet addressed the human elements that will make the greatest difference to your loved ones.

The good news is that you're not alone. Most people never move beyond basic legal planning, if they do any planning at all. By reading this book, you're already taking a critical step that many never do.

The TrueWealth approach will show you how to create a legacy that goes far beyond financial assets, one that will truly help your loved ones thrive for generations to come. You have the opportunity to become a parent, grandparent, or other elder whose wisdom and values will guide your family long after you're gone. Start by focusing on the fundamental building blocks in the coming chapters, and you'll be amazed at how quickly you can transform your legacy.

SCORE: 41-70

Some Basic Framework Exists, But the Human Connection Is Missing

You've taken important steps to prepare for the future, which puts you ahead of most people. However, you sense that something vital is missing in your legacy plans.

This feeling of incompleteness is common among those who have followed the traditional estate planning path. You've been told that having legal documents in place is sufficient, but deep down, you know there's more to leaving a meaningful legacy.

Your financial assets may transfer smoothly, but without the accompanying wisdom, stories, and love—your TrueWealth—your family could still struggle with the challenges that we saw the Wyatts face in Chapter 1. The good news is that you already have a foundation to build upon. The TrueWealth approach will show you how to become the family storyteller and wisdom keeper you aspire to be, supplementing your legal documents with the human elements your loved ones need most.

SCORE: 71-100

Ready to Refine and Deepen Your TrueWealth Legacy

Congratulations! You've already recognized the importance of both financial and human capital in your legacy planning. You're well on your way to becoming a conscious elder who thoughtfully prepares both material and spiritual gifts for your descendants. You're doing what most people never even consider.

At this level, your focus should be on refining and deepening the work you've already begun. Are there specific relationships that need more attention? Have you addressed both the practical and emotional aspects of your legacy? Could your documentation be more accessible or meaningful to future generations?

The TrueWealth approach will help you identify any remaining gaps and show you how to create a truly comprehensive legacy that will benefit your loved ones for generations to come. You're well-positioned to be that healing presence in your family line—breaking any negative patterns and establishing healthier ones—creating intergenerational wholeness that transforms your family's future.

As you review your assessment results, remember that creating your TrueWealth legacy is a journey, not a destination. Each step you take toward cultivating and sharing your wisdom, life stories, and love brings immediate benefits to you and your loved ones.

In the chapters ahead, I'll guide you through practical, proven approaches to creating a legacy that truly matters, one that will help your family thrive long after you're gone.

CHAPTER 2 TAKEAWAYS

- **Universal Need, Unique Expression:** The TrueWealth approach benefits everyone who cares about their family's long-term wellbeing, regardless of financial status, writing ability, or current family dynamics.
- **Present and Future Impact:** Cultivating your TrueWealth not only prepares for what happens after you're gone but transforms your current relationships in meaningful ways.
- **Beyond Legal Documents:** Traditional estate planning addresses what happens to your money and your stuff, but TrueWealth planning addresses what happens to your people—the values, wisdom, and love that truly constitute your legacy and help your loved ones for generations.
- **Family Identity Creates Belonging:** Sharing your wisdom and stories with future generations gives them a sense of belonging that research shows increases resilience and wellbeing.
- **Start Where You Are:** Whether you're just beginning to think about your legacy or have comprehensive legal documents in place, the TrueWealth approach will help complete your preparation in ways that matter most.

CHAPTER 3

THE HIDDEN COSTS OF TRADITIONAL ESTATE PLANNING

Now that you've completed your TrueWealth Legacy Assessment, you have a clearer picture of where your legacy stands. The assessment likely revealed some gaps that could rob your loved ones of the wisdom, connection, and belonging they desperately need to thrive–gifts only you can give, and only while you're still here. I've spent the last several decades working with families when a loved one passes away, and in this chapter, we'll explore the four major hurdles I consistently see that undermine even the most carefully crafted financial legacy, and most importantly how the TrueWealth Family Legacy℠ System specifically addresses each one.

HURDLE #1: THE SQUANDERING PROBLEM

One of the most painful realities for those who have worked hard to build wealth is the thought of having that wealth dissipate rapidly after they're gone. The statistics are sobering: approximately 70% of family wealth is gone by the second generation, and 90% disappears by the third generation. This pattern is so common it has earned a name: "shirtsleeves to shirtsleeves in three generations."

Research shows that 85% of failed wealth transfers are the direct result of passing on money without wisdom, values, stories, and the larger context that would have helped heirs. Those same studies show the other 15% of all wealth transfer failures could have been minimized.

The Reality of Rapid Wealth Dissipation

Last year my team took a call from the son of a client who had passed away just two weeks earlier. "Why can't you get me my money now?!" he yelled. "I've picked out the Maserati and they can only hold it until next week!" He was planning to spend $180,000 of his $200,000 inheritance on a car.

Unfortunately, this isn't unusual. I've seen inheritances that took decades to build vanish within months:

- A daughter who received $450,000 spent it all within eight months on vacations, designer clothes, and helping friends with their bills.
- Three siblings who each received $450,000 had nothing left after two years, despite having no major changes in their living situations.
- A grandson who used his entire inheritance to purchase an expensive boat that he later couldn't afford to maintain.

These aren't moral failings on the part of the inheritors. They're the natural result of receiving assets without also receiving the context, values, and wisdom that helped their parents and grandparents create those assets in the first place.

When most people die and the estate is wrapped up, their heirs receive a check. They deposit it in their bank account, maybe spend some right away, and then they go on with their lives, forgetting where the money came from.

Now, you might be thinking, I don't want my money to just be forgotten. I invite you to ask yourself why this bothers you. Why does it matter if they remember where it came from?

A lot of us feel that if they forget where it came from they're forgetting us, and we don't want to be forgotten when the money is spent. We don't want to be forgotten at all! We want to matter. We want to continue to help and shape and impact the lives of the people we love.

It's human nature to deposit an inheritance in the bank and then lose touch with where it came from. It's not a character flaw, it's because the estate planning system is set up to separate money from the people it came from. Someone dies, you read their Will to discover their wishes, you get a check, and you go on with your life. That's it, there's no connection between the money and the lives that were led and the sacrifices that were made to generate that money.

The system prioritizes the money and ignores every other facet of inheritance, including the people who made us and gave us the inheritance. It's not that most kids are shallow. It's the system.

But separating the money from the lives that created it also lessens the impact you and your money can have on your descendants, and I believe you want to have as much of a positive impact on them as you can.

So ... what if there were a way to bring the money and the people who gave it to us back together? To make sure the money will truly help your loved ones, and future generations?

How the TrueWealth Framework Helps You Overcome the Squandering Problem

The TrueWealth blueprint directly addresses the squandering problem by creating an unbreakable connection between financial capital and human capital. Rather than leaving heirs with just money, this approach ensures they receive the full context, values, and wisdom that created that wealth. This gives them the best chance possible at using it wisely and building their own wealth and financial independence to go with it.

The framework creates a comprehensive legacy system that transforms how inheritance is understood and received. Instead of seeing it as "money to spend," inheritors understand they're receiving part of a living legacy, complete with the stories, values, and hopes that give meaning to the financial assets.

This approach is unique because it doesn't try to control heirs through restrictive trust provisions or legal requirements. Instead, it creates intrinsic motivation through connection, understanding, and respect for what they're receiving. When an inheritor truly understands the lives lived and sacrifices made to create wealth, they naturally become more thoughtful stewards.

The framework also recognizes that financial literacy alone isn't enough. While many approaches focus solely on teaching money management skills, the TrueWealth system goes deeper by connecting financial decisions to family values, personal identity, and intergenerational responsibility.

Self-Assessment: What's the Status of the Squandering Problem in Your Life?

Take a moment to reflect on your current estate planning approach:

1. Beyond the legal documents in your estate plan, what have you communicated to your heirs about your values around money and wealth?
2. If your heirs received their inheritance tomorrow, would they understand the story behind that wealth? Would they know about the sacrifices, choices, and values that created it?
3. On a scale of 1-10, how concerned are you that your heirs might waste their inheritance? What makes you feel this way?
4. Have you ever had direct conversations with your heirs about your hopes for how they might use their inheritance? If not, what has prevented these conversations?

5. Have your loved ones had the financial literacy education they need to manage the money you will pass to them? Do they have a professional team in place?

If you're like most people, you've likely focused on the mechanics of wealth transfer—wills, trusts, and tax planning—but haven't addressed the human elements that determine whether your legacy actually endures. If you only plan for the mechanics of wealth transfer: wills, trusts, and tax planning, without addressing the human elements, your descendants will lose more than money, they'll miss the human capital that could have equipped them to build upon your foundation over the generations rather than deplete it.

HURDLE #2: THE EMPTY INHERITANCE PROBLEM

Cornelius Vanderbilt's grandson, Willy Vanderbilt, once said this of inheriting a substantial amount of money: "It has left me with nothing to hope for, with nothing definite to seek or strive for. Inherited wealth is a real handicap to happiness." This surprising statement reveals a truth that research has repeatedly confirmed: inheriting money without the wisdom that created it often leads to emptiness instead of fulfillment.

The Burden of Directionless Wealth

Psychological studies have shown that sudden wealth, whether from inheritance or other sources, frequently leads to:

- Increased anxiety and depression
- Strained relationships with family and friends
- Decision paralysis and fear of making mistakes
- Guilt about having unearned wealth
- Loss of purpose and motivation

One client told me about the overwhelming pressure he felt after receiving a substantial inheritance: "I kept thinking about how hard my parents had worked for this money. What if I made a mistake with it? What if I disappointed them? The money felt more like a burden than a blessing."

Traditional estate planning focuses exclusively on transferring financial assets efficiently. But something vital is missing—the transfer of your life lessons about finding purpose and meaning, experiences navigating life's challenges, wisdom from your challenges and mistakes, and values that provide direction for decisions.

Without these crucial elements, even substantial financial assets can leave heirs feeling empty rather than enriched.

How the TrueWealth Framework Helps You Overcome the Empty Inheritance Problem

The TrueWealth framework transforms a potentially empty inheritance into a fulfilling one by passing your wisdom, life stories, and love along with your wealth. Unlike traditional approaches that focus solely on asset transfer, this system creates a comprehensive legacy that includes your life's most valuable lessons about purpose, meaning, and fulfillment, and points your loved ones back to what matters most.

The framework enables you to map your life's journey, identifying pivotal moments that shaped your values and character. You can share not only your meaning and purpose, but how you arrived at them as well as the challenges and inspirations along the way. This creates a powerful connection between the wealth you've built and the experiences that made you who you are. It also serves as a lantern and map for your loved ones to live lives of meaning and purpose. Your heirs receive not just assets, but insights into the decisions, sacrifices, and principles that created those assets, and inspiration to pursue their own life's purpose.

Uniquely, the TrueWealth approach helps you reflect on what you inherited—both tangible and intangible—and what you wish you had received. This reflection ensures you break cycles of emptiness and support fullness for future generations. You can distill your key life lessons, share what you wish you'd known at different ages, and provide guidance for finding true purpose beyond material wealth. It also provides a structure to identify and lighten the load of those things that contributed to any emptiness you felt.

The framework also enables you to create milestone-based guidance that delivers wisdom exactly when your heirs need it most, at graduations, marriages, career transitions, or the birth of children. This ensures your mentorship continues even when you're no longer present.

What makes the TrueWealth framework even more powerful is having conversations with your children about their own values and how they foresee using the money they inherit, as well as your own values and any wishes you have regarding how they might use it? In this way you are able to rehearse and coach them on the handover of wealth and begin taking responsibility for it before it actually happens.

Self-Assessment: What's the Status of the Empty Inheritance Problem in Your Life?

Consider your current approach to legacy planning:

1. Have you documented the life lessons, values, and principles that guided your journey to success? Would your heirs know what truly brought you fulfillment?
2. If your heirs inherit your wealth tomorrow, would they receive any guidance about finding purpose and meaning in their own lives?
3. How clearly have you articulated what you hope your wealth will enable for your loved ones beyond material comfort?

4. Have you shared your insights about what brings lasting happiness versus temporary pleasure?

If you've primarily focused on the financial aspects of inheritance, your heirs may be set up for the very emptiness that plagues many who receive sudden wealth. Without the wisdom to find meaning and purpose, even substantial financial legacies can become burdens rather than blessings for future generations.

HURDLE #3: THE RELATIONSHIP BREAKDOWN PROBLEM

Perhaps the most heartbreaking consequence of traditional estate planning is what happens to family relationships after a loved one dies.

The Relational Cost of Sterile Legal Documents

Standard wills and trusts are designed to transfer assets, not improve or heal relationships, or prevent conflicts. Their cold, legal language can create an emotional vacuum at a time when families most need connection and meaning.

I've witnessed countless families torn apart after a parent's death:

- Two sisters who never spoke again after disagreeing about their mother's personal belongings
- Three brothers who spent fifteen years in litigation over their parents' estate, destroying relationships with each other and their children
- A daughter who interpreted her smaller inheritance as a final statement that her father loved her less than her siblings when, in reality, it was to account for money he'd given her during her lifetime

When we have tender or distant relationships, passing our TrueWealth is even more important. The best tool we have for cracking open generational traumas and patterns and creating family healing is to cultivate and share our wisdom, life story, and love.

How the TrueWealth Framework Overcomes the Relationship Breakdown Problem

The TrueWealth framework places healing and strengthening relationships at its center, fundamentally transforming how families navigate the transition of wealth and wisdom across generations.

Unlike traditional approaches that treat estate planning as a purely financial transaction, this system creates opportunities for deep emotional connection and understanding. The framework guides you through expressing your heart to each loved one—articulating appreciation, sharing cherished memories, offering forgiveness, and communicating hopes for their future.

The process encourages self-reflection about your journey as a parent or mentor. You're invited to examine what influenced your style, your struggles, and what you might do differently today. This creates space to explain your intentions and address any unintended impacts, opening doors for healing that traditional planning never considers.

A unique aspect of the TrueWealth approach is how it transforms sterile legal documents from potential sources of conflict into instruments of connection. The framework helps you explain not just what you're leaving to whom but why, providing context that prevents misunderstandings and hurt feelings.

The system also ensures the emotional significance of personal items is preserved. Rather than leaving loved ones to fight over possessions, you document the stories and meanings behind special items, turning potential points of conflict into cherished connections to family history.

And this process can make good relationships even better. Earlier, I told you the story of my neighbor Gene who described his relationship with his daughter as "fine" the day we first talked about her on our morning walk. Some gentle reflection on how much his daughter meant to him inspired changes in his behavior, which inspired changes in her behavior, and he now describes their relationship as "great!" They both started reaching towards each other and have a relationship today that wouldn't have happened if he'd stuck with the traditional plan of simply leaving her money via comprehensive legal documents.

Self-Assessment: What's the Status of the Relationship Breakdown Problem in Your Life?

Reflect on your current estate planning approach:

1. If you died tomorrow, would your estate documents bring your family closer together or potentially drive them apart? How confident are you about your answer?
2. Have you addressed any unspoken tensions or unresolved issues in your relationships?
3. For your closest relationships, have you documented what these people mean to you and what you specifically love about them? Would they know the depth of your appreciation and have a tangible way to hold onto it after you're gone?
4. Have you documented the emotional and historical significance of personal items that might otherwise be lost?

If your estate planning consists only of legal documents without emotional context or relationship reinforcement, you may not be passing what matters most to your family. Without intentional efforts to strengthen and heal relationships through your legacy planning, even the most carefully crafted legal documents fall short of strengthening the relationships we hold most dear.

HURDLE #4: THE LOST IDENTITY PROBLEM

When I was twenty-two, I was cleaning out my mom's house after moving her to a care facility due to early-onset Alzheimer's. Her house was piled high with clothes, newspapers, collectors' plates and stamps, and other miscellaneous stuff. Overwhelmed by the sheer volume of the belongings she'd been collecting, I spent weeks sorting through things before I finally threw the majority in the trash.

Years later I found out that those small metal pieces, the ones that looked like pins, with old, faded fabric on them? They were my Uncle Bob's Navy medals. He had served on the USS Arizona and was miraculously on leave when it was bombed in Pearl Harbor. He didn't have children of his own, so he left everything to his beloved little sister, my mom. All my courageous, loving uncle's personal belongings landed in a trash can because I didn't know his story, and I didn't know who I was: the niece of a Navy hero who lost most of his friends and shipmates one dark December day. That knowledge changes how I view myself and my own resilience and is worth passing down to my descendants.

The Cost of Lost Family Narratives

It's not just about your possessions. Research from Emory University has shown that children who know more about their family history have higher levels of emotional well-being and resilience (I'll share more details in the next chapter).[4] Yet traditional estate planning does nothing to preserve the stories and meaning behind the assets being transferred.

Carl Jung, the famous psychiatrist, said that having a connection to the generations—both those that come before and after us—gives us a sense of belonging, "rescuing us from isolation," and "restoring us to wholeness."[5] After all his years of study and practice, Jung believed this is the highest, best, and most important work we can do.

Recent research in epigenetics further underscores the importance of knowing our family stories. A few years ago, researchers did an interesting study. They took male mice and pumped the scent of cherry blossoms into their cages while giving them mild electric shocks on their feet. Two weeks later, they bred these mice. When those second-generation mice were exposed to the scent of cherry blossoms, guess what?! They became anxious and fearful. Their cortisol spiked. This reaction was seen not just in the second generation, but also the third.

Now, mice are pretty simple creatures, so maybe it's easy to understand how they could behave in such primal ways. But what about humans? Does epigenetics really carry our experiences from one generation to the next, too?

Consider this true story: One night, just after his 19th birthday, a young man named Jesse wakes up at 3:30 am freezing cold and terrified that if he falls asleep, he'll never wake up. This happens again every single night. After a year of this nightly ordeal, he drops out of college and forfeits the basketball scholarship he worked so hard to get.

Jesse meets with a therapist who asks if anyone in his family suffered a trauma that involved being cold, being asleep, or being 19. Surprisingly, shortly before this meeting, Jesse's mom had told him the story of how his uncle froze to death, in a snowstorm, at age 19. There was evidence in the snow that he had struggled to stay awake before he died. Incredible, right!?!

His uncle died three decades ago, and it was so traumatic for his family that they never spoke his name again. Now Jesse has been reliving this family story every night for a year. Once he sees that he's unconsciously taken on this old family trauma, Jesse is able to let it go and finally go back to sleep.

Epigenetics has shown us that some of our behaviors aren't chosen by us. Instead, some of the things we do and experience come from what our parents, grandparents, and great-grandparents experienced, carried by our DNA. That makes it crucial to understand our family stories so we can understand and become our fullest selves.

How the TrueWealth Framework Overcomes the Lost Identity Problem

The TrueWealth framework ensures your family's identity, stories, and heritage remain alive for generations. Unlike traditional estate planning that focuses solely on asset transfer, this approach creates a living tapestry of family narratives that give meaning to inherited wealth.

The framework guides you through preserving not just the facts of your life but the essence of who you are. You can document not only your own journey but also the stories of ancestors that shaped your family's identity. This includes recording family traditions, explaining the significance of cherished possessions, and sharing the values that guided your decisions.

A unique feature is the ability to capture your actual voice, expressions, and personality through recorded conversations. These might include dialogues between generations or personal reflections that allow descendants to truly know you, not just know about you.

The system also helps identify inherited patterns, both strengths and challenges, running through your family line. This gives descendants crucial context for understanding their own tendencies, gifts, and struggles, potentially freeing them from unconscious patterns that might otherwise hold them back.

Additionally, the framework transforms ordinary objects into treasured heirlooms by preserving their stories and significance. This prevents precious family connections from being lost, as happened with my Uncle Bob's Navy medals.

SELF-ASSESSMENT: WHAT'S THE STATUS OF THE LOST IDENTITY PROBLEM IN YOUR LIFE?

Consider your current approach to legacy planning:

1. If your heirs inherited your personal belongings tomorrow, would they know the stories and significance behind them? Would they recognize which items held deep meaning for you?
2. Have you documented your family's stories, traditions, and values in a way future generations can access and understand?
3. Do your descendants know the family stories that might be unconsciously affecting them—both the triumphs and the traumas?
4. Have you captured the essence of who you are—your voice, your personality, your unique way of seeing the world—for those who may never meet you?

If your legacy planning includes only financial documents without preserving your family's stories and identity, you're leaving a crucial void. Future generations may inherit assets but lose the connection to their heritage that could provide them with resilience, belonging, and a sense of wholeness that Jung identified as essential to human wellbeing.

Ultimately, true legacy transcends mere financial inheritance. It's about creating intergenerational wholeness, where wisdom and wealth work together to transform families and point them back to hope, purpose, and sustainable prosperity.

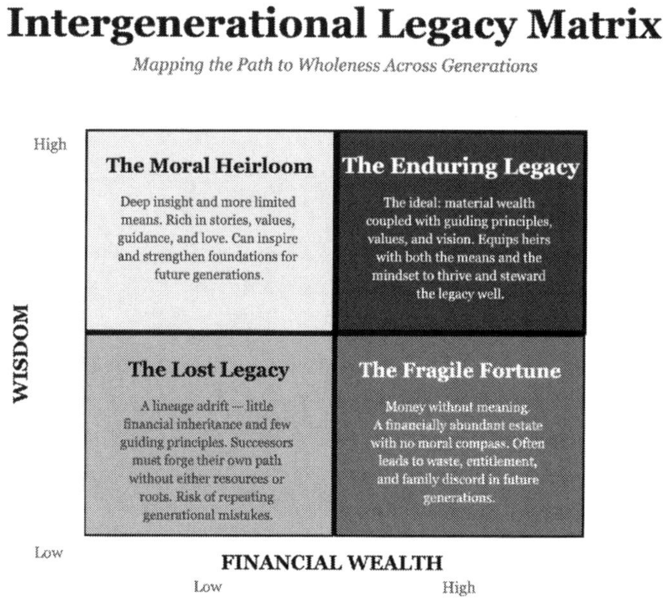

MOVING FORWARD WITH THE TRUEWEALTH FAMILY LEGACY℠ SYSTEM

The assessments you've completed reveal where the passing of your most important assets—your human capital—currently stands. If you identified gaps in any of these four areas, the TrueWealth Family Legacy℠ System provides the specific tools you need to address them.

Today you have the opportunity to pass on your TrueWealth to those you love. In the coming chapters, we'll explore exactly how to implement this system, ensuring your complete legacy nurtures your loved ones and creates the intergenerational wholeness you desire.

Whether you have significant financial assets or modest ones, your wisdom, life stories, and love are the true treasures your loved ones need. By integrating these elements with your financial planning, you create a legacy that truly helps your family thrive for generations to come.

Most people have no idea where to start in putting together their non-financial legacy, so I'll be walking you through everything that is needed in this book.

CHAPTER 4

THE SECRET KEY THAT UNLOCKS INTERGENERATIONAL THRIVING

When I stood in my mother's cluttered house sorting through the piles, I was searching for something. At twenty-two, cleaning out her home as she moved to a nursing home with Alzheimer's disease, I was looking for pieces of who she was—some way to understand her story. Why? Because I wanted to understand who I was.

Without knowing her story, or the story of any of my ancestors, I felt adrift, without an anchor in life.

This is precisely what happens when we don't pass on our TrueWealth.

After more than three decades of working with families, I've discovered a powerful truth: the secret to helping your family thrive for generations isn't found primarily in your investment portfolio or your legal documents. The most important element to your family's future thriving is found in three essential elements that most people never properly pass on: your wisdom, your life stories, and your tangible expressions of love.

ELEMENT #1: YOU MUST PASS ON YOUR WISDOM

The most dangerous thing about wisdom is that it dies with you, unless you intentionally pass it on.

Think about it: How many heartbreaks, financial mistakes, and career missteps did you endure before finding your way? Now imagine if your grandmother had left you a collection of her key lessons and principles, illustrated with personal stories. What if you'd had her lantern to guide you through those challenging moments?

Many people believe their wisdom isn't worth sharing. They think, "My kids aren't interested," or "My life wasn't that special." But as I've mentioned, research tells us that adult children consider your non-financial legacy ten times more important than your money. Your descendants need your wisdom, story, and love like plants need water.

The wisdom you've gained through your struggles is irreplaceable. Each financial crisis you survived contains lessons about resourcefulness and resilience. Every relationship that broke your heart taught you something about love, trust, and healing. Those career pivots and dead ends? They're full of insights about finding purpose and navigating change.

Your wisdom isn't just helpful, it's transformative. When my clients share their deepest lessons with their families, they often discover patterns they never noticed before. One client realized his seemingly different career challenges all stemmed from the same core issue: prioritizing others' expectations over his own values. This insight, passed to his children, helped them make career choices that aligned with their authentic selves from the start.

Financial advisors and family psychologists recognize this truth. They've seen firsthand how families with documented wisdom transfer fare better through economic cycles, relationship challenges, and life transitions. It's not just about having good advice, it's about having context-specific guidance from someone who shares your DNA (remember epigenetics from the last chapter?) and your family patterns. These might be the same people, or they might be different, and they're both important.

The Money + Wisdom Multiplier Effect

Here's what most people miss: when you combine financial inheritance with wisdom transfer, you create exponential impact. Money without wisdom often leads to the 70% wealth loss by the second generation that I spoke about previously. But money accompanied by the wisdom of how it was earned, lost, and rebuilt? That is a recipe for lasting prosperity. One family I worked with inherited not just their grandfather's real estate portfolio, but his proven principles for evaluating properties, handling tenants, and weathering market downturns. Three generations later they're still thriving, not just financially but with deep family bonds and shared values.

As my wise client Mark said, "In the relay race of life I want to pass the baton to the next generation. I don't want to drop it. If I did my job running and passing the baton, then they can do the same thing, pass the baton to their children, but do it their way."

How the TrueWealth Approach Makes This Easy

Instead of staring at a blank page wondering where to start, the TrueWealth Family Legacy℠ System breaks down wisdom cultivation into manageable pieces:

- Exercises that help you identify the deepest lessons hiding in your experiences
- Worksheets that draw out wisdom from each life stage
- Frameworks that transform your scattered insights into a cohesive guide your descendants can actually use

The process is designed to help you extract the gold from your experiences and package it so your great-grandchildren can apply it to their challenges, likely challenges you can't even imagine today.

Element #2: You Must Pass Your Life Stories

Your stories are more important than you realize. Your descendants need to understand your story, your parents' stories, and your grandparents' stories so they can begin to understand themselves. Your stories are important for several reasons.

We talked about the connection to the generations before us and after us giving us a sense of belonging. How many years did you spend looking for that sense of belonging in academics, sports, your profession, your marriage, and children? Yes, we all do that early in life, and sometimes well into adulthood. Having a connection to our ancestors helps us find that sense of belonging more quickly and more deeply. You are the only one who can give your descendants that gift of belonging from the outstretched arms of an ancestor.

I've heard Daniel Maté, son of renowned physician and trauma expert Gabor Mate, speak of this deep human need even in his own relationship with his father. He talks about how, without knowing his ancestors, he is lacking some crucial allies in his quest to become a whole person. And his father, Gabor, echoes this same longing, describing how he watches multigenerational families in parks with a sense of longing for the deep sense of belonging and comfort that comes from living within a multigenerational context.

And remember Jesse's story back in Chapter 3? He's the young man who couldn't sleep because he was reliving his uncle's story, one he had never heard of until more than a year after it started waking him up every night.

For more than thirty years, this trauma lived in the family's silence. Jesse was literally reliving his uncle's final moments every night because the story had never been told.

This is the power, and the danger, of untold stories.

Your life stories aren't just entertainment for future generations. They're the maps that help your descendants understand themselves. Knowing what our parents, grandparents, and other ancestors went through helps us understand ourselves and navigate successes, challenges, and losses using the wisdom gained by those who came before and the resilience that comes from knowing we are not alone.

It's important to share more than just the happy stories, the ones that show us in the best light and highlight all our strengths. The squeaky-clean version, edited and censored, does nothing to help your descendants at a deep level. If they think you were perfect and never struggled, they'll have a hard time accepting the imperfect parts of themselves. Our families need the version that shows who we really are.

Epigenetic research shows that trauma and resilience are passed down through our DNA. When you share your stories, you give your descendants the context to understand their own fears, strengths, and patterns.

Carl Jung said that connecting to the generations before and after us gives us a sense of belonging, and your stories create the connection he was referring to. They help your great-granddaughter understand why she feels anxious in certain situations. They show your grandson that his entrepreneurial drive isn't random, it's part of his heritage.

But here's what most people miss: it's not just about what happened. It's about how it affected you, how you overcame challenges, and what you learned. The time you lost everything and rebuilt? That's not just a tale of financial recovery, it's a blueprint for resilience. The relationship that broke your heart? That's a lesson in healing and self-worth for generations to come. And don't forget to share how you still struggle some days, that's what will help your loved ones relate to you as a human being and trust the wisdom you have to offer.

Family Narratives Build Identity and Resilience

As I mentioned in Chapter 3, research demonstrates that children who know their family's stories have stronger self-esteem, better emotional regulation, and greater resilience in facing challenges. Why? Because they understand themselves as part of something larger, a family narrative that includes both struggles and triumphs. This "intergenerational self" provides an anchor during life's storms.7

Future-Proofing Against Economic Volatility

In an era of increasing economic uncertainty, the resilience built through family stories becomes even more valuable. Families who know how their ancestors survived the Great Depression, navigated recessions, or rebuilt after losses are better equipped to handle financial challenges. This inherited resilience can be more valuable than any financial inheritance. It helps them retain more of the money they've inherited and use it more wisely.

How the TrueWealth Approach Makes This Easy

Most people don't share their stories because they don't know where to start or they think facts are enough. The TrueWealth system solves both problems:

- Tools that help you map your life chronologically, identifying key moments and drawing out the wisdom from your experiences
- Exercises that help you capture not just your stories, but how they shaped you
- Experiences to identify and gently share the challenges you or your ancestors went through that might be affecting your descendants through their DNA

Through this process, you're not just recording events, you're creating an intergenerational healing manual.

Element #3: You Must Create Tangible Expressions of Love That Transcend Your Lifetime

Leaving tangible reminders of your love can help carry your loved ones after you're gone and give your descendants a sense of belonging in a way that only you have the power to do.

Sarah, a client in her early forties, shared a story that illustrates this perfectly. Her mother had died suddenly when Sarah was in her thirties, leaving behind the expected money and material possessions that were divided among family members. But months later, while going through her old phone, Sarah discovered something priceless: a saved voicemail from her mom.

"It was nothing special," Sarah told me, wiping tears from her eyes. "Just Mom checking in, telling me about her garden, saying she loved me at the end, the kind of message I used to get all the time. But now, it's the only recording I have of her voice. I can hear her laugh, her slight Southern accent that got stronger when she was excited. I've saved it to three different devices and the cloud. I play it on her birthday and sometimes just on hard days."

That brief, ordinary message has become an extraordinary treasure, a tangible reminder of her mother's love that Sarah can experience over and over again.

Your loved ones don't just need to know you loved them, they need to experience that love in tangible ways long after you're gone: a letter gifted after your death, a video pre-recorded for a granddaughter's wedding, an audio message for when your loved ones doubt themselves, these become lifelines during life's storms.

The Lifelong Human Need for Parental Affirmation

Psychological research shows that the need for parental affirmation doesn't end in childhood, it continues throughout life. Even adults in their 60s and 70s report feeling deeply moved by discovering letters or recordings from parents who passed decades ago. This ongoing need for connection and validation transcends age and time.

Most of us feel this way, but we've been taught to ignore that longing. We can't ever get "enough" affirmation from our parents.

The Epigenetic Impact of the Expression of Love

Emerging epigenetic research demonstrates that emotional patterns, including feelings of being loved and valued, can be passed down biologically. When you create tangible expressions of love, you're not just providing emotional comfort; you're influencing the genetic expression of resilience and self-worth in future generations.

I've seen the power of these tangible expressions firsthand. Joe, in his 30s, told me the story of his grandfather's death and how he left behind love letters for each of his grandchildren. Rather than writing generic, blanket statements to all his grandchildren, he wrote two-part letters to each of them, individually. The first part instructed each grandchild to go to a specific place he named that was special in the relationship between that grandchild and the grandfather who wrote it. The second part was to be read by the grandchild in that special location, recounting their grandfather's memories with that grandchild, his love for them, as well as his hopes and dreams for their futures.

A young bride opened her deceased father's letter on the morning of her wedding, ten years after his death. She had been saving this letter for this day, just as he had instructed. In it, he shared his joy at imagining this day, his confidence in her choices, and specific memories of her strength and beauty. She told a friend later, "It was like he was there, walking me down the aisle."

Another family discovered their grandmother's box of "special occasion letters", one for each grandchild's high school graduation, college graduation, first job, wedding, and birth of their first child. These weren't generic congratulations. Each letter contained specific wisdom for that life stage, family stories relevant to the moment, and expressions of love tailored to each grandchild's personality.

How the TrueWealth Approach Makes This Easy

Creating lasting expressions of love feels overwhelming without guidance. The TrueWealth system in this book will give you:

- Letter templates with specific prompts that move you from "Dear child" to profound connection
- Preparation and guidelines for recording meaningful audio/video messages
- Frameworks for dealing with different relational circumstances
- Technological guidelines to help you get started

These aren't generic greeting cards—they're soul-to-soul transmissions designed to reach your loved ones exactly when they need you most. And if you'd like more help, you'll find upcoming workshops and retreats on our website at TrueWealthFamily.com

Self-Assessment: Your Legacy Readiness Score

Before we continue, let's check where you stand in preparing your TrueWealth legacy. Rate yourself on a scale from 1-5 (1 = not at all, 5 = completely):

	Self Rating (1-5)
1. I've documented the key lessons I've learned from my biggest successes and failures:	________
2. I've captured the stories behind my life's turning points, including how they affected me:	________
3. I've created tangible expressions of love for each person who matters to me:	________
4. I've documented family history and stories from previous generations:	________

5. I've shared the "why" behind my major life decisions with my loved ones: ________

Total Score: ________

20-25: You're well on your way to creating an extraordinary legacy

15-19: You've made a good start but have important work ahead

10-14: Your family is missing crucial pieces of your TrueWealth

5-9: Your human capital is at risk of being irretrievably lost

The Choice Before You

I've had several crux moments in my life, but one that stands out is the day in 2012 the bank manager called to tell me I didn't have enough money in my business account to cover payroll. Neither of us knew it at the time, but she was helping me build my legacy.

As I lay on my office floor believing that this time I'd truly run out of hope, that I might never be able to get my business back to profitability and as a result I might be ruining all of my employees' lives along with my daughters', I contemplated ending my life.

But as I lay on that carpet with tears streaming down my face, I remembered the times before that I'd felt like I was hopeless, and how I'd gotten through those moments, and decided to wait one day before I made any decisions. And, as had happened every time I'd felt desperate in my life before that day, I woke up in the morning able to feel a little more of the hope that existed in my situation despite the fact I couldn't feel it.

This moment has become part of my wisdom legacy, teaching my daughters, grandchildren, and great grandchildren in the future about resilience, about the temporary nature of despair, and about the hope that's always present even when we can't see it.

Every challenge you've faced, every lesson you've learned, every love you've felt, these are not just your experiences. They're your family's inheritance. The Maserati-buying son who called my office demanding his inheritance "now" needed his mother's wisdom and love more than the $200,000 he squandered as soon as he received the check.

Your descendants are searching for belonging in a world that feels increasingly disconnected. They're repeating patterns they don't understand, fighting fears they can't name, and missing the guidance only you can provide.

Psychiatrist Robert Jay Lifton's studies of Hiroshima survivors and how they were able to thrive after such devastation revealed that feeling part of a "collective life-continuity is a primal human need."8 What he's saying is that when those survivors lost everything, their families, homes, jobs, they found purpose in their lives again by looking back at previous generations and forward to future generations to find their grounding.

This is just as true for us and our descendants in whatever challenges life brings our way. Your wisdom, stories, and expressions of love create the collective life-continuity for which the coming generations have a primal need. They anchor your descendants in something larger than themselves. When our descendants discover ancestors who also went through a financial crisis or lost a child, spouse, or job and survived, they'll gain confidence that they, too, can make it through.

It helps them see the bigger picture and feel less alone in their challenges and pain. They have a deeper experience of hope, and none of us can ever have too much of that.

When Will We Need Our TrueWealth?

It's 4:00 on a Friday morning and my phone rings. I pick it up and see that it's my best friend, Carolyn, calling. My heart skips a beat, and I answer. Hello? Hello? Carolyn? And after a long 10 seconds her silence turns to sobs.

"They got the tests back. I have an aggressive leukemia," she says. "Without treatment, they think I have 6 or 7 weeks to live. I have to check into the hospital today."

This is the call we all dread, the one that changes everything. The one we know will come at some point, in some form.

She's 44, and up until now Carolyn has been the healthiest person I know. She eats clean, walks and runs daily, and she's a single mom with 3 kids at home.

Like most of us, Carolyn didn't get advance notice. But she's the kind of person who's prepared for everything. I mean, she Gets. Things. Done. When she checks into the hospital later that day, she doesn't have to scramble to get her affairs in order. Carolyn has spent her life clarifying and living by her values.

Now, she's an estate planning attorney so, yes, she has a comprehensive estate plan in place. But what's even more important is that she's already written letters to each of her kids, reminding them what they mean to her, what's most important in life, and how much she loves them. This frees her up to be fully present in each remaining moment, to focus her on her kids.

She lives longer than they expected, but never fully returns to her life at home. When she passes away, she knows that her kids will still have her love and guidance, even when her body is no longer here.

Carolyn left some money for her kids, but it's the TrueWealth she recorded and left behind that will serve as a compass and a lantern for them over the years.

The choice is simple but profound: Will you leave your family wandering without a map, or will you light the lantern that guides them home?

The TrueWealth Family Legacy^{SM} System transforms this overwhelming task into a step-by-step journey. It's time to stop hoping your loved ones will somehow absorb your wisdom or downplaying the value of what you have to offer and start intentionally passing on the TrueWealth that will help them thrive for generations to come.

CHAPTER 4 KEY TAKEAWAYS

- **The Three Essential Elements of TrueWealth:** True wealth consists of three vital components you must pass on: your wisdom, your life stories, and your tangible expressions of love.
- **Wisdom Is More Valuable Than Money:** Research shows adult children value the non-financial legacy from parents ten times more than money. The wisdom gained through your struggles becomes their shortcut to success. It's your wisdom, values, and love that have created your wealth in the first place, and it has the power to help your loved ones create and maintain their wealth, too.
- **Stories Create Identity and Resilience:** Your life stories aren't just entertainment—they're the maps that help your descendants understand themselves. Shared family narratives increase resilience and foster a sense of belonging.
- **Tangible Expressions of Love Become Lifelines:** Documented expressions of love like letters, recordings, and special messages become emotional anchors during life's storms, providing guidance long after you're gone.
- **The Multiplier Effect:** When wisdom, stories, and expressions of love accompany financial inheritance, they create exponential impact, protecting wealth from the common "70% loss by the second generation" pattern.
- **This Work Is Accessible:** The TrueWealth Family Legacy^{SM} System provides structured frameworks and support that make capturing and transferring these elements straightforward and manageable.

- **There Is a Limited Window of Opportunity:** We never know when the doors of communication will close. Creating your TrueWealth legacy now ensures your family receives this irreplaceable inheritance.

CHAPTER 5

THE INVESTMENT PROTECTION STRATEGY YOUR FINANCIAL ADVISOR NEVER TOLD YOU ABOUT

For nearly 30 years, I practiced estate planning the way everyone else did. I drafted wills and trusts, planned meticulous asset transfers, and implemented tax minimization strategies. I thought I was doing everything right, helping families avoid the legal headaches and heartaches I experienced with my mother's Alzheimer's and maximizing the money that passed to their children, until the day I realized I was only protecting half of my clients' legacies, and it wasn't the most important half.

The problem is, we don't see this until after my clients pass away, when I'm working with their families in the days, weeks, and years after their loved one died. That's where I see the impact of leaving money to your loved ones without the loving guidance that could make it more impactful.

Let's say you work hard for years, save up your hard-earned money, and on your 50th birthday you finally spring for your dream car. It's a Ferrari Testarossa, fire engine red. You've been driving for many years now, but once you pick it up at the dealership you realize it doesn't drive anything like the Lexus you're used to. When the first stoplight turns green, you gently press the gas pedal and instead of steadily accelerating you go jerking forward. You continue lurching and jerking all the way home, occasionally spinning the wheels, until you arrive home and park it carefully in the garage, hoping none of your neighbors witnessed your newfound inability to drive. You decide not to drive it until next Sunday morning when the roads are quiet, and you have some space.

You walk in the door, and your 16-year-old son asks if he can take it for a spin. He has a brand new driver's license and has been driving several times a week – in his Toyota Camry. He begs you, promising to be "very careful". You try to explain why he needs guidance and practice to drive the Ferrari, but he doesn't understand that it's more complex than the car he's used to.

It's not just that his inexperience could cause damage to the car, it could be downright dangerous for him to hop on the road in a car he doesn't know how to drive, for him and for everyone else.

That's exactly what most estate plans do,hand over the keys to someone who has little to no experience with the size, power, and complexity of the assets they'll be receiving. We regularly transfer financial assets to the next generation without transferring the wisdom and experience required to protect and grow them.

Sometimes this works out okay, and sometimes it doesn't. I've seen situations where an adult child is, unbeknownst to the parents, secretly self-medicating with drugs to try and cope with the stresses of life when their parents suddenly pass and leave them with a significant inheritance. What could happen to their drug habit in the absence of any affirmations of love left by their parent, and with suddenly a *lot* more money in their bank account?

I've seen other situations where the child becomes influenced by someone else to use the money in a way that is destructive, giving it to the person with negative influence or simply sending the adult child down the wrong path.

Over the last several decades I've seen many responsible, "good" adult children make decisions that they've regretted a few years later, and receiving their parents' wisdom and guidance could have saved them from learning those painful lessons with the money their parents worked hard for.

WHAT WE'VE BEEN TAUGHT ABOUT ESTATE PLANNING

When you think about estate planning, what comes to mind? Probably:

- Creating legal documents like wills and trusts
- Planning how to distribute your financial assets
- Implementing strategies to minimize taxes

These are the pillars of traditional estate planning, and they're what nearly every financial advisor and estate attorney will discuss with you. They'll ask about your bank accounts, investment portfolios, real estate holdings, and business interests. They'll create sophisticated trusts and develop complex tax strategies to maximize the money that your heirs will receive.

But here's the problem: This approach to estate planning is completely backwards.

Imagine you decide to take a trip. You've saved up money, you've planned the time off, now you want to make your travel plans. Would you start your planning by deciding on your mode of travel (whether you'll go by plane, train, or car) *before* you've chosen a destination? Of course not! Before we can choose the mode of transportation, we must decide where we want to go. Do we want to go to the grocery store around the corner, do we want to go to a nearby city, or do we want to go to Hawaii (or the continental U.S. if you are lucky enough to live in Hawaii)? Each of those destinations might require a different mode of transportation.

Where we want to go and what experience we want to create, for us and for our families, is what dictates our travel plans. Is this going to be a luxury vacation or are we going camping?

So, let's go back a step. Why do we do estate planning in the first place? What's the destination we want for our families?

We've been duped into thinking that the goal is passing our money to our loved ones when we're gone. But let's talk about that. If there's a fire in your house, and your spouse and children and sweet little dog are sleeping in the next room, but your coin collection and expensive painting are in another room, you're going to get your family out before you grab the coin collection and pricey painting … right?

Traditional estate planning only focuses on passing your financial assets. Your house, your bank accounts, your business, your retirement accounts. But those assets are not what's most important to you. The most important thing is your loved ones. And you'll be happy to know they feel the same way.

The whole purpose of wealth is to give our loved ones wellbeing. Most people lose the forest for the trees. After a lifetime of scrimping, saving, earning and accumulating wealth, we begin to believe an illusion that's who we are, that money is the end game. We forget that the real purpose of wealth is health, wellbeing and happiness. It's the opportunity to live well. The money is the vehicle, not the destination.

We take this illusion to the estate planning attorney, and they provide a way to preserve the illusion (the financial assets). But the money doesn't automatically give your loved ones happiness. In fact, it can do the opposite without your guidance. Money without guidance and love just fills up their bank account, rather than enhancing their happiness.

WHY THIS APPROACH IS INCOMPLETE–THE ROI PERSPECTIVE

Imagine building a beautiful house with top-grade materials, perfect architecture, and stunning design, but forgetting to add a roof. That's what traditional estate planning does to your legacy. It leaves your lifetime of experiences and wisdom exposed to the elements.

The 70% of wealth that's spent by your children, 90% of wealth that's gone by the next generation, and 30% of businesses that survive a transfer from one generation to the next aren't just numbers, they represent broken dreams, fractured families, and squandered opportunities.

The Hidden Costs of "Just Money" Inheritance

When wealth transfers without wisdom, several devastating patterns emerge:

Dependency: Beneficiaries often lose motivation to create their own success

Entitlement: "Easy money" creates expectations that life should always be easy

Family Conflict: Disagreements over money tear families apart

Poor Decision-Making: Without guidance, inherited wealth is often mismanaged

Consider this example: A wealthy entrepreneur passed away, leaving his children a profitable chain of restaurants. While he had carefully structured the trust and minimized taxes, he never shared his philosophy on customer service or his crisis management strategies. When a major health scare affected the industry two years later, the children panicked and sold the business at a significant loss because they didn't understand how their father had navigated similar challenges in the past.

And there's another example I've experienced, personally. The owner of my office building was an amazing landlord, responding quickly to requests, making sure the building services were excellent, and bringing holiday meals to every office. Sadly, he got sick and passed away unexpectedly. His family took over the building while his children were young adults, and client care and service have become afterthoughts. It's incredibly hard to get what we need, we can't get a response or get our office properly cleaned, and we are considering moving. Sadly, this family did not receive the wisdom from their husband and father that made him a successful property owner and developer over many years prior to his unexpected passing.

As a parent, I've had to walk the tightrope between doing too much for my daughters as they've launched into adulthood and not doing enough. I'm the kind of parent who wants to give my adult children everything I wish for them, and yet the last thing I want is for my love and support to hinder their own self-actualization. It's a dance we all do as parents of young adults, one that doesn't end when we're gone. It's incredibly important to pass my money to my daughters and grandchildren alongside my wisdom, life stories, and love because I want to save them from what they don't know yet because they've never had a large sum of money. And when it comes to my grandchildren, although they've got my heart wrapped around their precious little fingers, I'm still not looking to create entitlement.

WHAT I DISCOVERED AFTER 30+ YEARS AS AN ESTATE PLANNING ATTORNEY

Watching my clients' families after their loved ones passed away helped me see what was missing for me when my mom succumbed to Alzheimer's and was taken from my life. Seeing what's consistently missing for families, mine and many others, launched my journey to understanding what families truly need to thrive across generations.

Patterns Across Thousands of Client Families

Over more than three decades of practice, I've observed distinct patterns:

Families who transferred only money:

- Had higher rates of family conflict
- Carried a greater likelihood of wealth dissipation
- Experienced weaker family bonds across generations
- Repeated negative patterns (addiction, failed marriages, business failures)

Families who transferred their financial capital *and* their human capital:

- Enjoyed stronger family unity
- Carried out better financial stewardship
- Had higher rates of personal fulfillment
- Experienced the breaking of negative generational patterns

One family stands out. The patriarch built a successful manufacturing business but grew up in poverty. Instead of just leaving the business to his children, he documented:

- His decision-making framework for major purchases
- Stories of failures and what he learned
- The values that guided his business practices
- Letters to each child about their unique strengths

Three generations later, not only is the business thriving, but the family gathers annually to share new stories and lessons, continuing the tradition of wisdom transfer.

How You Transfer Your Wisdom Matters

There's a trend where companies now offer the public an opportunity to write their life stories, often through templated services that promise to preserve your legacy in book form. People are learning how important it is to leave more of themselves for their families. And while the intention is good, this approach falls short of creating a deep intergenerational impact. The fundamental flaw is that these biographical books are written before you've done any meaningful reflection. Without the excavation of values, lessons, wisdom, and love, these books become mere chronologies of events rather than transformative guides for future generations.

More importantly, a 200-page autobiography will not be read by most of your descendants. How many family members do you know who've actually sat down to read their ancestor's full life story when it was available, even if it's interesting? Beyond immediate family members, future generations who never knew you personally have little motivation to wade through decades of details to find the wisdom meant for them.

People are craving deeper connections to the generations who came before, but most companies are responding with tools that only scratch the surface.

The TrueWealth approach transcends these limitations by distilling your life's essence into purposeful, actionable formats. Through guided discovery and cultivation, you first uncover what matters most. Not just what happened, but what it means, how you overcame challenges, and how your hard-won wisdom can guide others. It is then packaged in digestible, targeted forms: legacy letters that can be read when your loved ones first receive an inheritance check, audio and video recordings that capture your voice and presence to be enjoyed during key life moments, values statements that guide financial decisions, a book with your hard-won life lessons and how you learned them, all in your handwriting, and specific stories tied to meaningful possessions or life transitions.

These focused formats meet future generations exactly where they are in their moments of need; a letter to read when facing their first business challenge, a video to watch before their wedding, or guidance recorded for when they become parents. Rather than hoping someone will mine a lengthy narrative for relevant wisdom, the TrueWealth process ensures your most valuable insights reach your descendants precisely when they'll be most receptive and in need of your guidance.

THE COST OF INACTION

Each day you delay documenting your TrueWealth is a day your family loses access to irreplaceable guidance. Consider:

The Emotional Price:

- Your children repeat your mistakes unnecessarily because they don't know your lessons
- Grandchildren feel unmoored, disconnected from the belonging that comes from knowing their heritage
- Family members struggle with decisions you could have guided

The Relational Price:

- Unresolved conflicts remain unhealed
- Unexpressed love stays unspoken
- Opportunities for deeper connection pass by

The Doors of Opportunity Will Be Closing One Day: As you read this book today, you probably have more time to think about what's important. Hopefully you have many more years to enjoy with your loved ones. But none of us knows how exactly much time we have. Each of us knows someone who passed away when their kids were still young or just when they were about to retire. I hope that you have more time, but it's never guaranteed.

I invite you to cultivate and record what matters most for your family now, while we know you're still here, so you don't have any regrets should life bring something surprising your way.

HOW TRUEWEALTH PLANNING ADDRESSES THESE LIMITATIONS

TrueWealth planning transforms estate planning by:

1. Integrating Financial and Human Capital

Instead of treating money and wisdom as separate, we recognize they're inseparable for true family thriving. Your financial legacy becomes exponentially more powerful when accompanied by:

- The principles that created the wealth
- The mistakes that taught valuable lessons
- The values that guide wise stewardship
- The expressions of love that will carry your family after you're gone

2. Providing Practical Tools for Implementation

We've developed specific tools and frameworks to discover, cultivate, and transfer:

- Your key life lessons through structured storytelling
- Your decision-making wisdom through guided exercises
- Your love and values through lasting expressions

3. Creating Support Systems for Accountability

Because this work is too important to leave to chance, we recommend that you partner with a friend or family member to keep moving forward with cultivating your TrueWealth. If you need more support, we also offer:

Workshops:

- Guided sessions and tools to discover, cultivate, and gift your TrueWealth
- Community support from others on the same journey
- Expert guidance to overcome common obstacles

1-1 Programs:

- Personalized guidance through the entire process
- Deep guided exploration of your unique legacy
- Creation of customized legacy documents and recordings

The choice is clear: You can continue with traditional estate planning and hope your family figures things out, or you can protect your lifetime of achievement and meaning by passing on the wisdom, stories, and love that transform money into true wealth. These are the things that have provided you with the wealth and wellbeing you have enjoyed. Give the next generation some of that.

Your financial advisor and attorney can help you minimize taxes. Your attorney can create perfect legal documents. But that won't give your children or grandchildren more meaning and purpose. Only you can pass on the human capital that ensures your family doesn't inherit just your money, they inherit your capacity to thrive.

The time to take care of your family is now. The doors of communication are still open today. Will you walk through them?

CHAPTER 5 KEY TAKEAWAYS

- **Traditional Estate Planning Is Backwards:** Most estate planning starts with financial assets and legal documents rather than family well-being and values, putting the vehicle before the destination.
- **The Protection Gap:** Standard estate planning leaves your legacy exposed by focusing exclusively on financial assets while neglecting the wisdom needed to protect those assets.
- **The 70/90 Rule:** Without wisdom transfer, 70% of wealth disappears by the second generation and 90% by the third, representing the failure of traditional approaches.
- **Hidden Costs of Money-Only Inheritance:** Dependency, entitlement, family conflict, and poor decision-making are the predictable outcomes when wealth transfers without wisdom.
- **Personal Experience Matters:** My journey through my mother's Alzheimer's revealed the irreplaceable value of human capital—the stories, wisdom, and love that can't be recovered once lost.
- **The Limited Opportunity:** The doors of opportunity to communicate our wisdom and love to future generations will close one day. We don't know how long we have, and it's important to remember to focus on what matters most while we still can.

- **Integration Is Key:** TrueWealth planning seamlessly combines financial and human capital, providing the complete protection strategy your financial advisor never told you about.
- **Support Systems Ensure Completion:** If passing your TrueWealth is important to you, the following chapters will help you get started. If you would benefit from more structure, our workshops and one-on-one programs provide the accountability needed to ensure this vital work doesn't remain undone.

PART 2

THE TRUEWEALTH FAMILY LEGACY SYSTEM

CHAPTER 6

THE TRUEWEALTH FAMILY LEGACY℠ JOURNEY PROCESS

In my work helping thousands of families navigate the transition from one generation to the next, I've noticed something profound. When people die, everyone gathers to share stories about the person's life. During the memorial service, one person after another steps forward to say, "Let me tell you what this person meant to me." They share specific memories, lessons learned, values witnessed in action. The kind of things each of us longs to hear from others.

Last year, I was moved by this dynamic when I attended the memorial service for a client's mother. Her daughter Sarah stood at the podium and said, "I wish she could hear what we're saying today." After the service, Sarah pulled me aside. "We prepared for everything else–the legal documents, the financial planning, even the funeral service. But we never had this conversation. All these beautiful things people are saying–she never got to hear them."

I don't know about you, but every time someone tells me how I've impacted their life or how much I mean to them it makes my day. It nourishes me at a level that nothing else can. *And yet, we save most of these loving statements for the memorial service, when our loved ones can no longer hear and be lifted up by them.*

I call this the Memorial Service Paradox. Many of us want to share our appreciation and feelings on a regular basis, but let's be honest: most family gatherings are made up of conversations about the potato salad, not the depth of our love and the specific ways our loved ones have impacted us. This is why we need a systematic approach to mining and transmitting our TrueWealth. Not just because it's efficient or organized, but because what matters most isn't what we bring up every day, when we're caught up in the moment. It's what emerges when we intentionally process our lives and relationships.

The Core Mechanism: A Systematic Approach to Mining Your TrueWealth

When I ask clients, "What do you want your children to know?" the first responses are usually surface level:

- "I love them"
- "I'm proud of them"
- "I want them to be happy"

These are true, but they don't have the power of what's beneath them. The transformative wisdom lies deeper, hidden beneath decades of unexplored experiences and love.

The human mind doesn't stay continuously focused on what matters most. We get caught up in daily rhythms, and the profound insights we've gained through years of living get buried under to-do lists and routine conversations. Without a systematic approach, we risk leaving our most valuable wisdom and what we treasure most about our loved ones unexcavated, unrefined, and undelivered.

The TrueWealth Family Legacy Journey has three phases: Discovery, Cultivation, and Gifting. Each phase transforms abstract wisdom into actionable legacy.

DISCOVERY: EXCAVATING HIDDEN TREASURES

During a recent Discovery session, I worked with James, a successful business owner in his seventies. When we began mapping his life journey, he started with the expected milestones: college graduation, first job, marriage, starting his business. But as we dug deeper into each life stage, something remarkable happened.

"Wait," he said, pausing over a period he'd marked as "challenging but necessary." "I just realized something. When I was twelve, my father lost everything in a business deal gone wrong. He was devastated. I remember finding him crying in the garage one night. From that moment on I became determined to understand business and money, so I'd never feel that helpless."

James had never connected that formative experience to his drive for financial education and business success. Now he saw it clearly: the boy protecting himself from his father's pain had become the man who built a thriving business. This wasn't just a story about success; it was about resilience born from vulnerability.

The Discovery phase includes:

- Mapping your life journey with intentional focus on transition points
- Identifying core values buried in difficult decisions
- Recognizing wisdom in both triumphs and struggles
- Understanding inheritance patterns (what you received and what you created)
- Extracting the stories and decisions that shaped who you are
- Discovering specific details behind your love for family members

And then there's Maria, whose father had passed when she was four. When we explored what she "didn't inherit but wished she had," she wrote: "A father's wisdom about navigating the world as a woman."

Later, as she drafted a letter to her own daughter, Maria realized she'd spent her entire life compensating for that absence by developing fierce independence and protecting herself. Now she could share both the lesson of resilience she'd learned and the vulnerability she'd carried. This transformation–from unexplored loss to transmitted wisdom–is the power of intentional discovery.

CULTIVATION: REFINING YOUR WISDOM, STORIES, AND LOVE FOR TRANSMISSION

Raw experience isn't wisdom–it's merely potential. During the Cultivation phase, we transform life experiences into actionable guidance.

As he reviewed his life stories, Robert, a recently retired engineer, kept saying, "I don't think my kids would find that interesting." His default was to edit out anything that felt ordinary.

But when he examined one "unremarkable" story more deeply, he uncovered gold. Robert had worked nights as a young father to support his family while his wife was ill. He thought this was just "what you do." But when we asked him to articulate what drove him during those exhausting years, he realized he was living out a belief: "Love is doing what needs to be done, especially when you're tired."

This wasn't just a story about working hard. It was a framework for love in action. We refined it further: "Love shows up consistently, even when it's costly, because commitment means placing another's needs alongside your own."

Suddenly, Robert saw this principle echoed throughout his life–in his marriage, his parenting, his friendships. This refined wisdom would now become something his children could apply to their own relationships.

Cultivating love requires the same intentional processing. During one session, I worked with Lisa as she prepared letters for her two daughters. When I asked what she loved about her younger daughter Emily, Lisa's first response was general: "She's creative and has a beautiful spirit."

But when I pressed for specific memories, Lisa broke into a smile. "When Emily was five, we had a huge fight about wearing socks. She hated them. I was at my wit's end one morning, trying to get her ready for preschool. Finally, she looked at me and said, 'Mama, my toes need to be free. It's how they breathe.'"

Lisa laughed, remembering. "In that moment I saw myself reflected back, my own stubborn independence and creative reasoning. I still had to get her to wear socks, but I fell in love all over again with her fierce certainty."

As we continued, Lisa discovered she could articulate exactly why she loved Emily's unique combination of creativity and conviction. This wasn't just "I love you"–it was "I love how you stand firm in your creative vision, even when it's inconvenient." This specific appreciation, once expressed, would become a cornerstone of Emily's self-understanding.

The Cultivation phase transforms:

- Experience into insight into transmittable wisdom
- Stories into frameworks for decision-making
- Regrets into guidance
- Accomplishments into values in action
- General appreciation into specific gratitude and love

Gifting: Delivering Your TrueWealth Strategically

The method of delivery matters deeply. My friend Carolyn, the successful attorney whose leukemia journey I shared earlier, made writing down her values and love for her children a priority even before she was diagnosed with a terminal illness. She wrote detailed legacy letters for each of her children–individual messages expressing her love, hopes, and values tailored specifically to each child's unique personality and needs. This is a gift that her children have for the rest of their days, the closest thing to having their mom with them.

Imagine taking this even further. What if, alongside written letters, you recorded video messages for your children to open at specific milestones? A son might receive a video to watch when he feels discouraged about his dreams, another for his college graduation, and a third on his wedding day. An audio recording could capture your voice as a grandmother, telling your favorite family stories, preserving not just the words but the warmth and rhythm of your storytelling. Or you can use a video to talk about how to navigate loss, telling the story of a loss you've endured, how you grieved and eventually moved forward.

You can record yourself reading your child's favorite bedtime story one last time or capturing advice about navigating the workplace that your daughter can access when starting her first "real" job. These multi-format gifts create layers of connection that bridge the gap between presence and absence.

The TrueWealth program does not dictate the form of your newly mined and wisdom. Most clients write letters. Many also record video messages, and some record multiple messages to cover specific events.

The Gifting phase considers:

- Multiple delivery methods (letters, videos, recorded conversations)
- Timing for maximum impact (now vs. future milestones)
- Individual versus collective messages
- Creating experiences, not just documents

The Science of Why this Process Works

Recent science confirms what wisdom traditions have always known: experiences and traumas transmit through generations.

The mouse experiment I mentioned earlier, where mice exposed to the scent of cherry blossoms paired with electric shocks passed deep anxiety about that scent to their offspring, illustrates how experiences literally change our DNA. Human studies show similar patterns. Descendants of Holocaust survivors show measurable changes in stress hormone regulation. Children of parents with PTSD are more likely to develop anxiety disorders.

But here's the breakthrough: passing our stories transforms the inheritance received through our DNA.

When Jesse, the nineteen-year-old who developed a paralyzing fear of falling sleep, finally heard the story of his uncle who had frozen to death at the same age and learned where his fear originated, understanding broke the cycle of inherited fear almost immediately. Once he saw the connection, he was able to release the unconscious pattern.

This is the power of processed wisdom versus unprocessed trauma. When we intentionally examine, understand, and transmit our stories, we transform potential trauma into strength.

Research from the previously mentioned Emory University Family Narratives Project shows that children who know their family stories demonstrate higher self-esteem, better emotional regulation, and greater resilience to stress. But the key factor isn't just knowing the basic storylines–it's knowing the complete stories, including the struggles that were overcome, and how. This helps children understand that life includes both triumphs and challenges and that they, too, can handle the ups and downs. The struggles we've overcome become the wisdom and encouragement that carries them through life's storms. When they know you've weathered a storm (or multiple), they know they can weather them too.

The Exponential Impact of Systematic TrueWealth Transmission

When I work with families through this process, I often return to the lantern metaphor. The wisdom you gently excavate becomes a light that guides your loved ones when you're no longer physically present.

Recently, an adult son shared how his father's letter–opened after his death–helped him navigate a crisis in his marriage. "Dad wrote about a time they almost divorced early in their marriage, and how they chose to fight for each other instead of fighting with each other. I had no idea they'd been through that. His words helped me see my own situation differently, and now that we've worked through those things I'm so glad I stayed in the marriage."

This is how cultivated wisdom transforms inheritance. Instead of receiving money that might be spent thoughtlessly, recipients inherit frameworks for living that inform financial decisions, relationship choices, and life direction.

These go beyond what we taught our children when they were young, when our focus was teaching them basic life skills and principles (and just getting them out the door with their shoes on!). And not only are they able to receive our wisdom at a deeper level as they get older, but we also have a lot more wisdom to share than we did when they were growing up. Our wisdom grows exponentially through adulthood, culminating long after our children have left the house. That wisdom doesn't have an opportunity to be shared in the average day-to-day life of a family whose children are out of the house and living their own lives, although this is when we have more wisdom to give. The older and wiser we get, the more intentional we must be about cultivating and sharing it.

My experience with families and the research agree:

- Children of families who share processed wisdom make more intentional financial decisions
- Recipients of legacy wisdom report higher life satisfaction and stronger family connections
- Grandchildren who receive transmitted wisdom show increased resilience and clearer sense of identity

Most powerfully, families who engage in this process report what Carl Jung described: a sense of belonging that "rescues us from isolation and restores us to wholeness."

The TrueWealth Family Legacy Journey isn't just about preparing for death. It's about living more fully now, with intention and meaning, knowing your love and life experience will continue to guide and bless those you love for generations to come.

CHAPTER 6 KEY TAKEAWAYS: THE TRUEWEALTH FAMILY LEGACY JOURNEY PROCESS

- **The Memorial Service Paradox:** We save our most meaningful expressions of love and appreciation for memorial services when our loved ones can no longer hear them, missing opportunities to nourish relationships while we're alive.
- **Surface vs. Deep Wisdom:** Initial responses about what we want to share ("I love them," "I'm proud") are true but lack the transformative power of deeper wisdom that emerges through systematic reflection and processing.
- **The Three-Phase Journey:** The TrueWealth process follows Discovery (excavating hidden treasures), Cultivation (refining wisdom for transmission), and Gifting (strategic delivery) to transform abstract insights into actionable legacy.
- **Stories Become Frameworks:** Raw experiences transform into actionable guidance when processed intentionally—Robert's "working nights while wife was ill" became the principle that "love shows up consistently, even when it's costly."

- **Trauma vs. Transmitted Wisdom:** Unprocessed family experiences pass down as trauma through DNA, but when stories are shared with understanding and context, they become sources of strength and healing rather than unconscious burdens.
- **Measurable Generational Impact:** Recipients of processed family wisdom make more intentional financial decisions, report higher life satisfaction, and demonstrate increased resilience, creating lasting positive change across generations.

CHAPTER 7

THE TRUEWEALTH FAMILY LEGACY℠ SYSTEM—STEP BY STEP

Through the previous chapters, you've discovered that cultivating and leaving your human capital is just as important as earning and passing on your financial capital, and can have a deeper, more lasting impact. Now it's time to transform this realization into tangible gifts for your loved ones through the TrueWealth Family Legacy℠ System.

This systematic approach isn't about perfection; it's about authentic connection. It's a gentle excavation of your life's treasures that enables you to share your real self, not just your highlight reel. The careful layering of discovery and your willingness to look at and share the ups and downs of your life make the entire system work. In this chapter, I'll share a detailed description of the process and some of the why behind the specific steps and exercises we will be using to cultivate and pass on your TrueWealth.

STEP 1: DISCOVERY

Discovery begins with creating sacred space in your life to explore where you've been in life and who you've become. This isn't just an intellectual exercise, it's also about letting yourself feel your way through your story.

Mapping Your Life Journey and Experiences

You'll explore your life's pivotal moments—both the celebrations and the crucibles. This process invites you to trace not just what happened, but how these experiences shaped your values, stretched your capacity, and revealed your true strength. You'll discover patterns you never noticed: how every major transformation began as an ending, or how your greatest fears became your most powerful teachings.

Many people discover surprising threads of resilience woven through their challenges. After completing some of the exercises in the Discovery phase, one client had an experience common to this phase of the TrueWealth process. She looked at the map of her life experiences and noticed several events she described as "breakdowns". After each breakdown, she saw something positive was created. For the first time, she could visually see that her breakdowns also became breakthroughs. This recognition transformed what previously seemed like random events into purposeful chapters of her becoming, and important lessons to pass on to her loved ones. This perspective arises regularly through the TrueWealth system as you begin to look at your life map and experiences in light of your generational legacy.

Discovering Your Key Stories and Life Lessons

Within your life's experience lie stories that carry unique power; moments that shifted everything, choices that revealed your character, encounters that expanded your understanding. This part of discovery involves recognizing which experiences contain wisdom worth preserving. Not every story needs telling, but some demand it. You'll learn to identify which memories hold transformative potential, which struggles birthed unexpected strength, and which joys reveal your deepest values.

The process invites you to see your life as a teacher sees it, looking for the lessons hidden in the living. During this phase, we invite you to tell and re-tell the stories related to the experiences from the map in the previous step/phase. Have you noticed how your stories change just a little each time you tell them? Or that the stories you tell from years ago have different meaning as you age and see them in the light of your growing wisdom? In the Key Stories and Life Lessons phase, we are using language to re-tell the stories from your life to align them and coordinate them with your wisdom. Most clients love this phase because they get to re-tell their stories and align them to their values. It feels fun and light; you get to discover how you're the real and courageous hero in your own life story.

It can also be awkward and uncomfortable because when you begin looking at the arc of your life, your stories don't yet have the themes that hold them together. As you tell them, the themes begin to emerge. You are a natural born storyteller. And your deepest values and wisdom want to be celebrated, cherished and especially shared. This is the first step where clients tell us they are seeing themselves and their life more deeply and begin to have a deep sense of purpose and satisfaction in cultivating their human capital.

Janine and her husband had the cruise of a lifetime planned right before they separated. Janine, a self-described frugal person, would be damned if she was going to lose the deposit on that trip. So she did the hardest thing she's ever done and not only went on that cruise alone but created "new friend quotas" for every day on the trip. She transformed that cruise from what could have been a sad experience into a new social group who she still vacations with today.

But that story didn't become a success story until she realized, years later, she was cruising with the same friends for the third year in a row.

Try on old stories with a new perspective. How do they shift? Try telling a new and different story. This is a playful approach where the language you use can be delightful, surprising and instructive. What if she didn't actually leave you all those long years ago? What if you had to go? What if that wasn't the worst thing ever, but led to the best thing ever? How would that change the story?

A simple conversation with a stranger might have changed your direction. A mistake you thought would define you negatively might contain your hardest-won wisdom. Through gentle reflection, these key stories emerge as the ones that can truly guide your loved ones, offering not just information but illumination for their own paths.

Uncovering the Wisdom Beneath Your Stories

Once you've identified your key stories, the real treasure lies in excavating the wisdom they contain. This process involves looking back through time with compassionate clarity, asking yourself what you wish you had known at pivotal moments. What understanding could have eased your twenty-five-year-old self through career uncertainty? What perspective might have helped you navigate relationships more skillfully? What truth about resilience could have steadied you during your darkest hours?

This exploration reveals two types of wisdom: the hard-earned insights you gained through experience, and the understanding that only comes with hindsight. You'll discover wisdom about handling failure, building relationships, finding purpose in struggle, and maintaining hope when circumstances seem hopeless. These aren't just life hacks—they're the profound realizations that emerge when you view your past through the lens of survival and growth.

This phase is one of my favorites, and it requires patience. Your inner wisdom has a way of emerging naturally. Insight is common as you take your time in this step. We hear "Oh my goodness!" a lot when people finally see the wisdom below the stories that are connected to core beliefs and values.

We have a natural tendency to want to rush the insights, as if it's an equation of sorts: input the experience, receive the wisdom. But it's less linear. Pay attention to your thoughts while driving or showering. We recommend things like yardwork during this process, ways to keep your hands busy but that let your mind wander.

This step relies on your natural desire to connect your life to meaning and wisdom. It's there, even if it's buried beneath the surface. And when you "see" how a story connects a theme in your life with a nugget of wisdom, it is one of the most rewarding experiences you can have. It's like a corner puzzle piece in your life finally falls into place and you begin to see the picture of your life much more deeply and with more meaning.

The wisdom uncovered here becomes the most practical gift you can offer your descendants: a compass and road map for navigating their own journeys with greater clarity and courage. Rather than beginning their life's race at the starting line, you can hand them the baton of your insights and hard-won lessons so they can avoid a few of the potholes you fell into.

Identifying What You Inherited and What You Wish You Had

Another exercise in the TrueWealth Family Legacy℠ System is the What I Inherited exercise. In this phase, we are connecting the life stories from our map, and the inherent wisdom from those stories to our place in the long arc of the generations in our family. We do this because we want to consider our lives in relation to what we gift to future generations. It gives us context and perspective, without which we might miss crucial generational experience. We are interested in passing along the helpful parts of our generational history without ignoring some of the more difficult aspects of intergenerational giving.

You'll take a look at what you received—and didn't receive—from previous generations. This exploration includes tangible inheritances like family treasures, intangible ones like character traits and beliefs, family patterns—both helpful and unhelpful—and the gaps where desires or crucial needs went unmet.

This process reveals both the treasures you want to make sure you carry forward and the patterns to consciously transform. Your gentle excavation continues as you identify which inheritances serve your descendants and which cycles need weeding out.

The most important part of this exercise is discovering what you wish you had inherited but didn't. This gives you key areas to focus on as you pass forward to your own descendants and loved ones.

Clarifying Your Core Values and Principles

You'll distill the principles that have truly guided your life; not the ones you think you should value, but the ones you've lived by in your most authentic moments. These values emerge through reflection on your hardest decisions, your proudest moments, and the convictions you've held through adversity.

Your essential values become the compass guiding every legacy decision, ensuring that what you pass on reflects who you truly are.

The Personal Transformation That Begins with Discovery

Something profound happens when you honestly explore your life's landscape. People often experience revelations: "I never connected these dots before" or "I see my struggles differently now." The discovery process itself becomes healing as you realize you're not just recording history, you're recognizing and rewriting the meaning of your life's experiences.

This shift from cataloging events to discovering purpose in the Discovery phase creates the foundation for everything that follows.

Discovery Exercise: The Hidden Thread Think of a difficult period in your life that you rarely talk about. Write down one specific moment from that time when you made a choice that surprised even you. What does this choice reveal about who you really are?

STEP 2: CULTIVATION

With discovery complete, cultivation transforms raw experiences into refined wisdom. This stage requires deepening your embodied truth-telling while maintaining the gentle excavation rhythms that allow you to look at the entirety of your life's journey without judgment or getting stuck in the hard parts.

Mining Your Wisdom and Life Lessons

In the cultivation phase, you'll select significant experiences and extract their essential teachings. This isn't about teaching your morals through parables—it's about sharing what you genuinely learned through living. You'll explore not just what happened, but what shifted in you as a result.

When processing challenges, many discover unexpected gifts. From her life map, Jeannie catalogued a history of financial struggle stories during the time when she and her husband were raising their two sons.

When reflecting on these stories and re-telling them from today's wisdom point of view, she saw that she and her husband valued financial independence and hard work. She immediately recognized that she wanted to express that value to her grandchildren.

As she cultivated these stories further it surprised her that underneath those stories of financial hardships, she and her husband always cherished the family and their time together.

Jeannie casually recalled one of these stories of a budget road trip, sharing it with one of her sons and they got a good laugh. She was truly humbled when her son told her that those hardships and their focus on the family relationships taught him to value people over material things. This became one of her most treasured legacy messages.

This is the winding route towards finding your story's meaning, purpose and wisdom preparing you to gift what's most meaningful to you.

Processing Unresolved Issues and Deepening Relationships

The cultivation process naturally brings unfinished business to light. Perhaps it's unspoken appreciation, unexpressed forgiveness, or acknowledgments long overdue. Your gentle excavation allows you to address these at your own pace and readiness. There is no set timeline, and we recommend taking plenty of time to process as you cultivate your human capital, while continuing to take steps forward on a regular basis.

You'll have opportunities to identify what's incomplete, whether that's making amends where you unintentionally hurt a family member, releasing old grudges, or finally thanking someone who changed your path. I work with couples one-on-one as they discover what's left undone and the freedom and peace of mind they find when they take even small actions to find closure. This healing benefits you immediately while creating cleaner legacies for your descendants.

Preparing Your Stories and Messages

You'll transform experiences into narratives your loved ones can truly receive, in formats that are engaging and digestible. This isn't about crafting perfect tales—it's about authentic sharing that honors both your humanity and their capacity to receive complex truths.

You'll learn to distinguish between telling stories in a way that heals and instead of burdens, creating messages that empower rather than overwhelm.

How Cultivation Brings New Purpose and Vitality

This is the part of the TrueWealth process where people consistently say they feel more alive than they've felt in years. There's profound energy in realizing your struggles weren't random, they were preparing you for this very act of giving forward. In cultivating our human capital, we also clarify what's most important to us. Then, we spend our days taking meaningful action towards more of what we truly want.

This sense of purpose can revitalize entire family systems, creating ripples of hope through generations.

Exercise: From Story to Wisdom Take the moment you identified in Discovery. Complete this sentence: "Because of this experience, I now believe that ...". Then refine it into practical guidance by asking: "How would I explain this belief to someone I love who might face something similar?"

STEP 3: GIFTING

The final phase of the TrueWealth Family Legacy[SM] System is Gifting, where you transform your cultivated wisdom, life stories, and love into tangible expressions for your family. Here, both embodied truth-telling and gentle excavation ensure authenticity without overwhelm. We will explore embodied truth-telling in detail in Chapter 8.

Choosing the Right Vehicles for Your Legacy

You'll select from various options: written letters, recorded conversations, video messages, wisdom collections, future-milestone gifts, personal music or art, or any other expression that reflects you. The key is matching the vehicle to your authentic voice and your loved ones' ability to receive.

Some choose traditional written letters, while others create multimedia experiences. What matters isn't the medium, but the truth carried within it. And research shows that recording your voice has a meaningful impact on coming generations, so

I recommend that you include some form of audio and/or video to express yourself to those you love. The TrueWealth system has basic suggestions on how to get started which I share in coming chapters and in our workshops and one-on-one work with clients.

Creating Tangible Expressions of Your TrueWealth

The creation process itself can become meaningful family time. Some of our clients use this process to create new and lasting memories with their wisdom and stories, while simultaneously recording them. If your grandchildren are the right age, you could ask them to interview you. You can give them some questions to ask you and also have them come up with a few questions that interest them. You might involve children in selecting photos for a legacy book, or have children interview grandparents about life lessons. These collaborative moments often become cherished memories themselves.

Remember: authenticity trumps polish. Genuine wisdom shared imperfectly resonates more deeply than perfect packaging without heart. Perfectionism has ruined many good intentions for me. Your family doesn't want to see the "polished you", they want to see the "you" they came from.

Sharing Appropriately During Your Lifetime and After

You'll gain discernment about what to share now versus what carries more power when discovered later. Some expressions of love and encouragement enhance relationships immediately. Other deeper teachings might serve better when needed during life transitions.

Through the TrueWealth process, you'll have the opportunity to identify what gifts you want to pass on now and which ones you'll pass later. A general principle I hold is that sharing is most effective now, because there's more time for it to benefit your loved ones in the context of their lives. And a letter that you leave to be read after you're gone, or videos you record specifically to be gifted in your absence, can add to the foundational legacy you've already passed on.

This timing wisdom emerges through your genuine connection to each recipient's current needs and capacity.

Digital Legacy Considerations for Modern Families

Today's families need both traditional and digital legacy components, and through the TrueWealth Family Legacy℠ System you'll consider how to preserve and transmit your TrueWealth through technological tools while ensuring the human essence remains central.

This includes practical considerations like digital asset management alongside the deeper questions of how technology can serve, not overshadow, your legacy's heart.

A More Powerful Inheritance

What you have the opportunity to leave your loved ones is a family inheritance guidebook. Picture this: when it's time to distribute your estate, instead of simply receiving a check, your loved ones get the check along with a letter where you tell them how much they mean to you, specifics of what you love about them, and your long-term goals for how you hope this money will help them.

You share what you were like at the age they'll be inheriting, and what you wish you had known back then, along with your hopes and dreams for their futures.

Perhaps you leave a journal with the words "Mimi's Big Book of Wisdom" across the top, with the hard-won lessons you hope will make life a little easier for your loved ones, including a dose of your unique style of humor.

Maybe you set up rules for their inheritance, maybe not. But either way, you leave love and guidance along with the money, so it's much more likely that the money will be spent well.

You've also written a letter to be opened when your grandson gets married or has his first child, when your niece or great-granddaughter graduates. It doesn't matter which occasions you honor, what matters is that your loved ones now have tangible ways to feel your presence and love.

And along with everything you've put in writing, your loved ones discover audio and video messages you left just for them, or songs you wrote, drawings with symbols or family jokes that they'll immediately recognize, customized games, or books of poetry about your life and family. You can be creative and use whatever best reflects who you are.

Exercise: The Perfect Moment Choose one person you love. If you could sit with them during a moment when they really needed encouragement, what would you want them to know about how you see them? Write those specific words down. This is the beginning of your gift to them.

The Two Key Strategies That Make TrueWealth Work

Throughout this three-step process, two essential strategies ensure success:

1. Community Support: This means not walking this journey alone. When reflecting on transformative moments, having trusted companions—whether family members, friends, or organized groups—provides perspective, encouragement, and accountability. A supportive community creates a mirror that helps you see yourself more clearly and a sounding board that deepens your insights. This shared experience enhances the authenticity and impact of your legacy gifts.

2. Gentle Excavation: Like carefully revealing buried treasures, this approach prevents overwhelming yourself or your loved ones. You maintain respect for your readiness to explore difficult terrain, knowing the work unfolds in its right timing. This gentleness creates safety for honest exploration and creates space for deeper wisdom to emerge.

Together, these strategies transform the TrueWealth process from a task into a sacred journey. They ensure what you leave behind isn't just documentation but transformation.

Your legacy isn't about having all the answers, it's about offering your authentic journey forward as a foundation and beacon of hope. When you combine the wisdom of community with gentle excavation, you create something that genuinely helps your loved ones thrive.

Here's what I've seen first-hand: cultivating and passing on your TrueWealth will change the way your descendants use your money, it will change who they become and how they navigate the obstacles they face, and it will change every day we have left on this earth.

And if you're stuck, TrueWealth has programs that will help you get through the process step by step at TrueWealthFamily.com.

CHAPTER 7 KEY TAKEAWAYS: THE TRUEWEALTH FAMILY LEGACY SYSTEM–STEP BY STEP

- **A Systematic Approach Transforms Abstract Love into Actionable Legacy:** The three-phase TrueWealth system (Discovery, Cultivation, Gifting) provides a proven methodology to excavate your life's wisdom and transform it into tangible gifts that create intergenerational wholeness.
- **Discovery Reveals Hidden Patterns and Purpose:** Through intentional life mapping, you'll uncover surprising threads of resilience and meaning that connect your experiences, transforming what felt like random events into purposeful chapters of your becoming.
- **Cultivation Refines Raw Experience into Transmittable Wisdom:** Stories become frameworks for decision-making when processed intentionally. A father's "working nights while wife was ill" transforms from mere hardship into the principle that "love shows up consistently, even when it's costly."
- **Strategic Gifting Creates Lasting Connection Across Time:** The delivery method matters deeply, whether through personalized letters, milestone videos, or recorded conversations, strategic gifting bridges the gap between presence and absence, ensuring your wisdom reaches loved ones when they need it most.

- **The Process Breaks Generational Cycles Through Understanding:** When family stories are shared with context and understanding, they transform from inherited trauma into sources of strength, turning unconscious patterns into conscious healing that benefits generations to come.

CHAPTER 8

MAKING PEACE WITH YOUR WHOLE STORY

INTRODUCTION: THE WEIGHT OF PARTIAL STORIES

Most families operate on carefully curated versions of their histories, sharing only what feels safe, comfortable, and acceptable. We've learned to "stay positive" from an early age, to present our best faces to the world. This well-intentioned practice, while understandable, has a profound cost for authentic legacy.

Many of us haven't felt comfortable embracing the full truth about our family histories. Why would we, when acknowledging certain realities might make us, or those we love, appear weak, imperfect, or flawed? Or when sharing them brings up feelings we'd rather not experience again? The fear of how family conversations might unfold keeps us hesitant. What if they see us differently? What if opening old wounds causes more pain than healing? Often, we don't even realize how much remains unshared across generations because these gentle omissions have become normal.

These silent gaps don't just prevent authentic legacy, they create intergenerational confusion. Descendants wonder why certain challenges keep emerging in their lives when they have no awareness of similar patterns in their parents, grandparents, or great-grandparents. The missing pieces get buried deeper with each generation that maintains the partial narrative.

The "everything is fine" performance exhausts families at a deep level. It requires constant mindfulness to maintain appearances, to remember what can and cannot be mentioned, to keep stories consistent and certain chapters closed. But this weariness has deeper implications that ripple through generations.

You cannot be a "wise ancestor" without reflecting on and sharing your complete journey. Your descendants will face real and challenging situations too, perhaps surprisingly similar to ones you navigated. The wisdom they most need is precisely what you discovered through your difficulties, what you consider your struggles or learning moments. By keeping these private, you leave your descendants to rediscover hard-won insights you already unearthed through experience.

WHAT HONEST REFLECTION MEANS IN LEGACY WORK

In the context of TrueWealth, honest reflection isn't confession, it's completion. It's not about unburdening yourself onto family members or seeking validation for past actions. Instead, it's about completing the unfinished chapters that live within your family story.

Authentic sharing in legacy work is about transforming experiences into wisdom. When we can reframe our most challenging moments into meaningful narrative, they become vessels for insight rather than sources of ongoing discomfort. This shift invites us to see our lives as chapters in a larger family book, not isolated incidents of personal struggle.

Consider Margaret, who initially resisted exploring her divorce, calling it "ancient history that doesn't matter." But the TrueWealth life mapping process helped her recognize that her experience of rebuilding after betrayal had become the foundation for her strength in later challenges. With the support of the structured reflection questions, she was able to identify the specific wisdom she'd gained: "Healing happens in layers, not all at once, and that's okay." This insight became one of her most treasured legacy gifts to her granddaughter facing relationship struggles.

The distinction between honest sharing and overwhelming others with raw experience is essential. Overwhelming others dumps unprocessed emotion and events onto recipients. Thoughtful sharing, however, offers insights wrapped in context, timing, and consideration. It asks: "What purpose does this serve? How might this help? How can I share this in a way that heals rather than burdens?"

There's wisdom in approaching complete stories with compassion. When applied to legacy work, this freedom shows up as release from the tiring effort of maintaining partial narratives. It allows both the sharer and listener to stop wondering what's missing, to understand patterns that seemed puzzling, and to give meaning to struggles that felt without purpose.

THE THREE LAYERS OF FAMILY UNDERSTANDING

Family understanding exists in layers, each inviting different kinds of courage to explore.

Surface understanding encompasses the facts everyone acknowledges: dates, places, major life events that form the outline of family history. We moved, changed careers, celebrated milestones. These stories are generally comfortable to share because they exist in the external world where details are straightforward.

Unspoken understanding comprises the experiences we quietly avoid. These are the events that shaped us deeply but remain unmentioned: the relative who disappeared, the real reason for financial trouble, challenges that were labeled differently, or difficult childhood experiences. These stories invite tremendous gentleness because embracing them shifts familiar patterns.

Deeper understanding represents patterns we don't always recognize. The way certain emotions express themselves similarly across generations, how specific concerns seem to skip a generation only to reappear, why particular topics remain untouched without anyone remembering why. These insights invite not just gentleness but perspective, often with help from others to see patterns we're too close to notice.

Each layer invites its own form of courage. Surface understanding invites openness. Unspoken understanding invites vulnerability. Deeper understanding invites wisdom.

THE HESITATION AROUND COMPLETE STORIES

The greatest barrier to honest reflection often stems from our care for relationships. We imagine that sharing challenging stories will damage connections we've worked hard to build. This concern, while understandable, often overestimates the fragility of genuine relationships and underestimates their capacity for healing through honesty.

We tell ourselves we're sheltering others from "unnecessary difficulty." But this protection often denies them context that would explain their own genuine experiences. When descendants struggle with patterns they can't understand, they see themselves as responsible for what are, instead, inherited dynamics as if something is "wrong" with them.

Another common hesitation stems from our desire to protect our loved ones from pain. We tell ourselves that sharing certain realities (addiction in the family, mental health struggles, financial crises, relationship failures, mistakes we made that still weigh us down with guilt) would only hurt them unnecessarily. "Why burden them with this?" we ask. "They don't need to carry this pain."

But this well-intentioned protection often backfires, creating more confusion and pain than the truth would have caused.

When we hide significant parts of our story, our loved ones may blame themselves for family patterns they can't understand. A daughter wonders why she struggles with anxiety when no one in her "perfect" family ever seemed to have mental health challenges. A son feels ashamed of his financial mistakes, unaware that his father faced similar struggles and found his way through them. A granddaughter repeats relationship patterns without understanding their roots in family history.

Our silence, meant to protect, often leaves descendants feeling isolated in their struggles and questioning whether something is fundamentally wrong with them. The protection we think we're providing by hiding difficult truths instead deprives them of context, connection, and the wisdom that could help them navigate their own challenges with greater understanding and self-compassion.

The familiarity of family narratives provides a peculiar comfort. "Our family has always been resilient." "We don't talk about those things." "Parents are in charge, and children should do what they say—and not disagree—no matter their age." These stories, while limiting, offer predictability in an unpredictable world. Exploring beyond them means breaking longstanding family patterns and possibly making people uncomfortable, including yourself.

Perhaps the deepest hesitation emerges from wondering "What will they think of me?" After decades of thoughtfully managed presentation, revealing complete stories feels like standing before those whose opinions matter most. This hesitation touches our core desires for belonging and acceptance within our family circles.

Another core concern for clients is the desire to focus on positivity, not giving more attention to the "negative" in life. Many of us have been coached throughout our lives to "think positive" and "focus on the good things." This well-meaning advice has been amplified in recent decades by happiness studies, motivational speakers, and spiritual teachings about gratitude and optimism. We've internalized the message that dwelling on difficult experiences is unhealthy, unproductive, or even spiritually immature.

"Why focus on the negative?" we ask ourselves. "Shouldn't I let the past be the past?" This hesitation reveals our fear that honest reflection means giving painful experiences more power in our stories. What we don't realize is that acknowledging the pain and challenges from the past doesn't magnify their impact, it actually helps free and release it, turning undefined shadows into specific moments with beginnings, middles, and ends that no longer hold us captive. When we can name and place what was difficult, we often discover it occupies less space in our lives than when we spend energy keeping it hidden.

True positivity isn't about absence of difficulty; it's about integrating all experiences into a meaningful whole, giving them space to breathe and to move so they're no longer stuck like ghosts in our memories. This freedom changes our lives, and those of our descendants, in ways we could never have anticipated. When you feel free, you release the real parts of you that never felt safe to be fully expressed before now.

How the TrueWealth Process Creates Safety for Complete Stories

The TrueWealth process recognizes that uncovering complete stories requires both courage and support. Unlike trying to navigate this journey alone, the systematic approach provides scaffolding that makes honest reflection both safer and more productive.

The Discovery phase begins with structured life mapping exercises that gently guide you through your experiences without forcing premature exposure of sensitive material. You're not asked to immediately share your most vulnerable moments; instead, you're invited to notice patterns and themes that emerge naturally as you trace your journey.

During Cultivation, the process provides specific frameworks for processing difficult experiences before sharing them. This isn't about "getting over" challenges, but about finding meaning and wisdom within them. The guided reflection helps transform raw pain into processed insight, making sharing purposeful rather than simply cathartic.

Many clients find that working through the structured exercises reveals connections they'd never noticed—how a childhood challenge developed resilience that served them throughout life, or how a family struggle taught lessons about perseverance that their descendants desperately need to hear.

APPROACHES TO HONEST REFLECTION

Authentic reflection in legacy work begins with self-awareness exercises from your TrueWealth journey. As you explore life mapping, inheritance patterns, and core values, themes emerge that prepare you for deeper sharing.

Choosing what to share with whom invites thoughtfulness. Not every story needs sharing with every family member. Consider each person's readiness, the potential positive impact, and what would be most helpful. Some insights might be best preserved in legacy letters to be discovered later, while others can be shared directly when the timing feels appropriate.

David felt overwhelmed when he first considered his father's alcoholism as part of his legacy work. The TrueWealth process didn't push him to immediately craft a story about it. Instead, the inheritance exploration exercises helped him recognize that his father's struggle had taught him about compassion, boundaries, and the importance of seeking help. The structured approach gave him time to process these insights privately before deciding how to share them with his own children.

Timing considerations matter deeply for sensitive stories. Sharing during celebrations, stress periods, or when recipients are managing their own challenges can overwhelm rather than heal. Choose moments when there's space for reflection and conversation for all people involved.

One of the biggest reasons not to share now is when you know that the reaction you will receive will cause you additional pain or frustration. In my family, there are stories that I choose not to fully share with certain family members because sharing these things is more hurtful than helpful to me. This is not just a hunch or a fear after one difficult conversation, it has played out over many conversations and years, testing the waters again periodically. I have family members who are not ever going to be able to witness the pain that their actions caused nor create space for me to express myself without their defensiveness and there's no benefit in sharing more with them now.

The experience of sharing versus receiving stories in legacy work involves different considerations. Sharing insights invites preparation, context, and gentleness. Receiving stories calls for openness, patience, and often, the ability to hold space for the sharer's feelings as they open up.

STRUCTURED SUPPORT WITHIN THE TRUEWEALTH FRAMEWORK:

- **Life mapping with gentle pacing:** The discovery exercises allow you to explore your timeline without pressure to immediately process or share everything
- **Values clarification as a foundation:** Understanding your core principles first provides a lens for interpreting difficult experiences constructively
- **Story selection guidance:** Not every story needs telling; the process helps you identify which experiences contain wisdom worth preserving
- **Processing before sharing:** Built-in reflection steps ensure you've found meaning in experiences before attempting to transmit them to others

- **Multiple delivery options:** The gifting phase offers various ways to share sensitive stories, from private letters to guided conversations, allowing you to choose methods that feel safest

FINDING CLARITY WITHIN

Before sharing insights with others, you will want to embrace them yourself. This means being open to noticing your own blind spots, the narratives you've maintained that may not fully align with reality or your true values. The TrueWealth exercises often reveal these, gently but consistently.

TrueWealth work also exposes them kindly. It asks you to discover where you didn't do as well as you wanted to and rather than "beat you over the head with it again" it asks gentle and reflective questions like where else has this shown up? What are the patterns with this mistake or regret? How can I mine those patterns into wisdom to pass along? How can my descendants learn from my mistakes?

Exploring your inheritance patterns becomes like carefully uncovering layers of understanding about yourself. What patterns did you absorb that you haven't acknowledged? What cycles do you see repeating in your relationships, parenting, or life choices? These recognitions prepare you for broader family sharing.

Looking honestly behind the curtains of your family's "official story" might be the most challenging part. One powerful technique we use is to reflect honestly and non-judgmentally on your own parenting. Where did you continue inherited patterns you hoped to change? What impact did your unresolved experiences have on your children? This self-reflection isn't about self-criticism, it's about completion and wisdom.

Clients find the freedom of embracing their complete journeys is liberating. When you can view your life with honesty and kindness, seeing both achievements and learning moments as part of a whole path, you model for your descendants that their complete stories are valuable too.

This was beautifully illustrated by Margaret, who had always described her mother as "strong and independent." It was a family badge of honor. During her life mapping exercise, however, she realized this narrative had gaps. "My mother wasn't just strong; she was afraid of vulnerability," Margaret wrote. "She never let anyone help her, even when she was struggling."

This realization hit Margaret hard. "I've been doing the same thing, refusing help, trying to handle everything alone. I thought I was being strong like Mom, but I've been exhausting myself trying to live up to an incomplete picture."

Margaret began exploring what true strength might look like, one that included accepting support when needed. She wrote her reflections in a letter she never intended to send but found healing in writing: "Dear Mom, I understand now that some of what I admired in you was also what hurt inside you. I'm learning to be strong enough to be vulnerable."

When Margaret's daughter came to her during a difficult divorce, Margaret shared both her mother's approach to hardship and her own evolving understanding. "My mother never showed weakness, and I followed her example for years. But I'm learning there's strength in reaching out when you need help." Her daughter burst into tears. "I've been trying so hard to handle this alone because I thought that's what you would expect."

"That conversation changed our relationship," Margaret shared. "By seeing the full picture of my mother's strengths and limitations, and my own, I gave my daughter permission to find a different way."

SHARING WITH YOUR CLOSEST CIRCLE

Begin conversations with those most open to listening; perhaps a sibling who's always been understanding, a spouse who already knows much of your journey, an adult child who's matured enough to hold life's complexities, or a trusted mentor.

The gentle power of beginning with "I've been reflecting on..." or "I've recently understood something about myself..." creates curiosity rather than defensiveness. These phrases suggest contemplation rather than confrontation, discovery rather than criticism.

Creating emotional comfort before sensitive sharing is essential. This might mean agreeing on privacy, asking for a pause when emotions arise, or having a caring third party present to maintain a supportive environment.

The TrueWealth Family Legacy[SM] System is designed to give you the best opportunity to uncover your wisdom, meaning, and purpose. During this process we guide you through looking at patterns in your family. Some of our clients come up against resistance within themselves or within their families that could best be navigated and resolved with professional support. Rather than seeing this as derailing the process and giving up, clients who create powerful and successful legacies by passing their TrueWealth continue with the journey while seeking professional help to dig deeper into some of the more emotionally charged experiences and patterns.

Sometimes professional guidance becomes valuable, especially when exploring deep challenges, family patterns, or situations that might affect many relationships. Therapists, family guides, or spiritual advisors can offer neutral space and skilled support.

FEELINGS AND EXPERIENCES THAT MAY SIGNAL NEED FOR PROFESSIONAL SUPPORT:

Overwhelming Emotional Intensity

- Feeling flooded with grief, anger, or trauma when exploring family patterns
- Experiencing panic attacks or severe anxiety when confronting family stories
- Finding yourself unable to function normally after certain discoveries about your past

Family Trauma Responses

- Uncovering patterns of addiction, abuse, or neglect that feel too heavy to process alone
- Discovering family secrets that challenge your entire understanding of your identity
- Feeling responsible for "fixing" generations of family dysfunction

Relationship Crisis

- Family members becoming hostile or cutting off contact when legacy conversations begin
- Spouse or children expressing feeling judged or criticized by the process
- Long-buried family conflicts erupting when stories start being shared

Identity Overwhelm

- Feeling completely lost about who you are when examining inherited patterns

- Experiencing what feels like an identity crisis: "If this pattern isn't really me, then who am I?"
- Becoming paralyzed by the weight of responsibility for future generations

Resistance That Feels Stuck

- Finding yourself consistently unable to move forward despite wanting to
- Feeling trapped between honoring your family and breaking unhealthy cycles
- Experiencing what feels like self-sabotage whenever you try to cultivate your wisdom

You will know that you need support when you feel genuinely overwhelmed, stuck, or unable to process what you're discovering in a way that feels healing rather than harmful. Professional support can provide the safe container needed to navigate these deeper waters while still honoring the transformative goal of creating intergenerational wholeness.

BRIDGING GENERATIONS WITH UNDERSTANDING

Sharing patterns that influenced your parenting invites profound honesty. Perhaps you continued your parents' cautious approach or responded in ways that created different challenges. Discussing these patterns, especially with your children, calls for humility and gentleness.

Offering wisdom from your struggles often provides more practical guidance than your achievements. How you learned from setbacks teaches more valuable life skills than how you reached successes. How you found peace with inherited worries offers more hope than if those concerns had never touched your family.

Moving past the "ideal ancestor" image invites others into reality. When you embrace your moments of doubt, worry, or searching, you allow descendants to acknowledge theirs. They need to know you as a real, whole person who also made mistakes. You become relatable rather than distant, and real ancestors offer real guidance.

Daniel Mate, son of Gabor Maté, the famous physician and trauma expert, has shared that what he most longs for from his own father is not telling him what to do but sharing about his own life, and giving him guidance from within the context of 'I've been there, too.'

Authentic sharing creates healing across generations by shifting patterns of silence. When you can say, "I found my way through this because others in our family faced it too, and here's what I discovered," you change patterns that might continue without awareness.

TRANSFORMING STORIES INTO WISDOM

Reframing family challenges into family strengths happens when stories are shared with understanding and learning. The relative who "went their own way" might reveal someone pioneering new approaches to living. The ancestor who "faced many trials" shows herself as someone navigating unprecedented circumstances. Giving context transforms confusion about a family experience into clarity.

Open stories become guideposts when shared thoughtfully. "I learned this lesson the gradual way" provides direction your descendants can use when facing similar crossroads. These stories offer both caution and encouragement—you can learn deeply and still create meaning.

Creating space for your descendants to be authentic, too, might be the greatest offering of honest sharing. When you model openness you welcome others to lower their guards, too. Family gatherings can become places for genuine connection rather than careful performance.

The comfort of "I'm not alone in this" spreads through generations. When cousins discover shared experiences, when siblings speak about common childhood moments, separation transforms into unity. Family becomes a source of strength rather than tension or shame.

When James first started his TrueWealth journey, he hesitated to include anything about his father's alcoholism. "I don't want my kids to think less of their grandfather," he explained. "He was a good man who struggled with a disease."

During our work together, James gradually recognized that his father's struggle had shaped his own approach to life in profound ways. "I became hypervigilant about keeping commitments because my dad was so unpredictable. I never wanted my children to feel that uncertainty."

When James finally shared this context with his adult children, his son had a revelation. "Dad, I've always wondered why you get so upset when plans change at the last minute. It makes so much sense now." This insight transformed what had been a source of tension and shame between them into a moment of deep understanding between father and son.

James later told me, "By sharing that part of my father's story, and my response to it, I didn't diminish his memory. Instead, I helped my children understand both him and me more completely. And my son realized his own discomfort with uncertainty might have roots deeper than his own experience."

This story demonstrates how sharing family truth with compassion can create intergenerational healing. James gained profound insight into both his grandfather's humanity and his own inherited patterns around uncertainty, moving the family from unconscious trauma to conscious wisdom. Through honest storytelling, three generations shifted from disconnection and confusion to connection and clarity.

TrueWealth is a system that helps people learn, recognize, and use the right tools to turn any pain you've experienced into wisdom for the benefit of future generations.

WHEN SHARING FEELS CHALLENGING

Working with family members who aren't ready to look at or discuss the truth about experiences you or others in your family had calls for patience. You can't encourage others to embrace understanding before they're prepared. Your role is to share your insights and remain open to conversation when they feel ready.

Honest reflection has thoughtful boundaries. Some stories might involve others' privacy, contain sensitive details, or risk unnecessary hurt without clear benefit. Wisdom appears in recognizing when sharing serves growth and when it serves other purposes.

Creating legacy materials when relationships remain strained needs special gentleness. Letters can be written to distant family members with warmth rather than reproach. "Should you read this someday, things between us may not have healed, yet I want you to know..." offers bridge-building even beyond time.

Sometimes honest reflection becomes a future gift. By documenting complete stories in sealed legacy documents, you provide understanding for coming generations when current ones cannot receive it. These time-released gifts can bring healing decades after they're prepared.

One of my favorite stories about just such a time-released wisdom gift is the story of Robert, whose estrangement from his youngest son had lasted nearly a decade when he began his TrueWealth work. "I don't even know where he lives now," Robert admitted. "How can I create a legacy when part of my family won't speak to me?"

During his exploration of his family patterns, Robert recognized how his own father's emotional distance had shaped his parenting. "I thought providing financially was enough, that's all my father did. I never learned how to talk about feelings or apologize when I was wrong."

Robert decided to write a legacy letter to his estranged son, unsure if he would ever be able to deliver it. In it, he acknowledged the family patterns he had continued unwittingly, expressed his regret, and shared the wisdom he had gained too late for their relationship: "I mistook silence for strength and provision for love. I know now that wasn't enough."

Two years later, Robert received an unexpected phone call. His daughter had found the letter among Robert's papers while helping settle his affairs during a health scare and mailed it to his son. "He told me he wasn't ready to rebuild a relationship, but he appreciated understanding where some of my limitations came from," Robert shared. "It was a small opening, more than I expected."

Robert's experience demonstrates how honest reflection can create healing even when reconciliation seems impossible. "I had to make peace with my story first, including my mistakes, before I could offer anything useful to my son. Whether he ever fully accepts it or not, I know I've done what I can to break the cycle."

When you "clean up your side of the street", no matter how others respond, you have the joyful experience of living on a clean street. Your life feels better before the message has even been delivered. And imagine the power of delivering the message at just the right time.

THE RELIEF AND LIBERATION OF AUTHENTIC LEGACY

Honest reflection brings ease to legacy creation. When you're not constantly editing, weighing, or filtering your journey, the process becomes natural. You're simply sharing experiences as you've lived them, insights as you've discovered them.

The distinction between gifting assets and gifting understanding becomes clear through authentic reflection and sharing. Assets are what you transfer, and they have a finite impact. But the understanding gained through honest reflection is what you carry forward, carrying the power to transform generations of lives. Honest reflection ensures you share wisdom and lived experience rather than just facts or possessions.

Building an environment of acceptance for coming generations might be your most lasting legacy. When they witness you engaging honestly with life's complexities, acknowledging learning moments, and healing from difficulties, they understand they can do the same. They don't need to perfect their journeys before claiming their place in the family narrative.

Authentic legacy outlives idealized legacy because it supports descendants' actual lives. The filtered version of family history offers little guidance for meeting real challenges. The honest version, rich with lessons and recoveries, provides the guidance they truly need.

The Safety of Community in Story Work

The TrueWealth approach recognizes that complete stories often emerge more safely in community settings—whether in formal groups, with trusted friends, or through guided conversations with family members. When we attempt honest reflection in isolation, we can become overwhelmed by emotions or stuck in old patterns of thinking.

Community provides perspective that we cannot achieve alone. Others can reflect the wisdom they hear in our stories, helping us recognize insights we might miss. They can also offer gentle challenges when we're minimizing our experiences or avoiding important connections.

Many clients find that sharing their discovery and cultivation work with a trusted friend or group creates accountability that keeps them moving forward while providing emotional support for the more challenging aspects of the journey.

GENTLE APPROACHES TO HONEST REFLECTION

Conversation beginnings that welcome openness:

- "I've been thinking about some family patterns..."
- "I recently understood something that might help explain..."
- "There's an insight I'd like to share that brought me clarity..."
- "I've discovered something about myself that connects to our family..."

Writing approaches for sensitive stories:

- Write as if sharing with a caring friend
- Create a timeline of events, then layer in feelings and understanding
- Compose letters you may keep private to explore your perspective
- Separate facts from emotions, then blend them gently

Creating comfort in family conversations:

- Begin with shared gratitude
- Agree on consideration for all involved
- Include natural pauses
- Close with acknowledgment of family bonds
- Practice good listening skills
- Keep tissues and comfort items nearby

Approaches that honor life's richness:

- Include multiple viewpoints on meaningful events
- Provide context letters that explain timing of sharing
- Create "introductory pieces" that prepare readers for deeper insights
- Use supplementary sections for stories that need additional care

Embracing complete stories in legacy work isn't about revealing everything but about creating genuine connection. It transforms family history from a managed narrative into a living source of wisdom, healing, and possibility. When you choose to share honestly, first with yourself then with your family, you offer the ultimate gift: the freedom to be fully human, fully genuine, and fully cherished.

If you'd like more guidance or support in cultivating and sharing your whole story, I work one-on-one with a few families a year. Visit TrueWealthFamily.com to apply.

CHAPTER 8 KEY TAKEAWAYS

- **Authentic Legacy Requires Complete Stories:** You cannot be a "wise ancestor" without reflecting on and sharing your complete journey, including both triumphs and struggles, as this is where your most valuable wisdom resides.
- **Partial Stories Create Intergenerational Confusion:** When family members only share sanitized versions of their experiences, descendants lack context for understanding recurring family patterns, their own struggles, or seemingly "irrational" behaviors.
- **Honest Reflection Transforms Pain into Wisdom:** The process of examining your complete story—with gentleness and compassion—transforms raw experiences into meaningful guidance that can help future generations navigate similar challenges.
- **Breaking Cycles of Silence Creates Healing:** When you courageously share processed insights about family patterns and challenges, you give descendants the tools to understand themselves and potentially break negative cycles rather than unconsciously repeating them.
- **Authentic Sharing Builds Stronger Connections:** Relationships deepen when family members can move beyond "everything is fine" performances to genuine understanding, creating space for real human connection across generations.

PART 3

GETTING STARTED WITH TRUEWEALTH PLANNING

CHAPTER 9

BEGIN WITH THE FAMILY LEGACY ROAD MAP

The journey of a thousand miles begins with a single step.

- Lao Tzu

"I don't even know where to start with my personal legacy."

This is what Linda told me when we first sat down together to discuss her legacy. A successful business owner in her early sixties, Linda had plenty of financial resources to leave to her children and grandchildren. She'd already updated her Living Trust and other documents multiple times over the years.

But something felt incomplete.

"I want to make sure they know who I really am," she said, "not just what I owned. I want them to know how much I love them, and to pass on what I've learned, usually the hard way. But I don't know what's most important to say to my family. And how do I organize it all?"

If you're feeling like Linda, you're in the right place. In this chapter, we're going to take that crucial first step together. The Family Legacy Road Map is designed to help you get a birds-eye view of what matters most in your legacy journey. It's a way to organize your thoughts and identify the areas where you'll want to focus your attention in the coming chapters.

The best part? You can complete it in a single sitting and immediately feel a sense of clarity and purpose about your TrueWealth legacy.

UNDERSTANDING YOUR STARTING POINT

Before embarking on any journey, it helps to know where you are. When using GPS to navigate to a new destination, the first thing the system does is locate your current position. Your legacy journey works the same way.

Assessing What You've Already Done

Take a moment to acknowledge where you are and what you've already accomplished. Perhaps you've created a will and/or trust, designated beneficiaries for your accounts, and purchased life insurance. If you haven't yet gotten the legal documents in place, here's your reminder that these are vital to make things as smooth and easy as possible whenever your time comes. See Appendix A for information on the primary tools you need to have in place.

As to your human capital, you will also want to assess where you are and the legacy you've been creating over your lifetime. Maybe you've already had meaningful conversations with loved ones about your values or written letters to be opened after you're gone.

All of these actions are valuable pieces of your legacy. The Road Map exercise will help you see how they fit together and where there might be gaps to fill.

Robert and Jeanine, a couple in their seventies, were surprised when they realized how much groundwork they'd already laid. "We thought we were starting from scratch," Jeanine told me, "but when we listed everything out, we saw that we'd been building our legacy in small ways for years. We just hadn't connected the dots."

Identifying Priority Areas

Everyone's legacy journey is unique. Your priorities will depend on your family situation, your values, and the specific wisdom and stories you want to pass on.

For some, like my client Miguel, preserving family traditions was paramount. "My grandparents brought these traditions from Mexico," he explained. "I want my grandchildren to understand why we celebrate certain holidays the way we do, why we make these specific foods. It's not just about the traditions themselves, it's about the values they represent."

For others, like Alicia, a single mother of two, documenting life lessons was the top priority. "I had to learn everything the hard way," she told me. "If I can spare my kids even a few of the hard knocks I went through, that's what matters most."

The Road Map will help you identify what matters most to you.

CREATING YOUR PERSONALIZED TRUEWEALTH VISION

Before diving into the specifics of your legacy, let's take a moment to think about the big picture. What does success look like for you? What impact do you hope your legacy will have on your loved ones and future generations?

Defining Success for Your Family Legacy

I often ask my clients to complete this sentence: "I will know my legacy has been successful when..."

The answers are as varied as the individuals themselves:

"...when my grandchildren face challenges and think, 'What would Grandma do?' and find strength in the stories I've left them."

"...when my children use their inheritance to create opportunities for others, not just themselves."

"...when future generations feel connected to their family history and understand how it has shaped who they are."

"...when my life's lessons and values continue to influence family decisions long after I'm gone."

Your definition of success will be unique to you and your family. The Road Map will help you articulate it clearly.

Setting Specific Goals for Each Recipient

Not everyone in your life needs the same things from your legacy. Your adult son who struggles with financial decisions might benefit most from your wisdom about money management. Your teenage granddaughter might treasure stories about your own adolescence and how you navigated challenging times.

Tom, a retired teacher, created different legacy packages for each of his three children. "My oldest son already knows most of my stories—he lived through a lot of them with me. But my youngest was born later, during a more stable time in our lives. He never saw the struggles. I want to make sure he understands where our family values of perseverance and gratitude came from."

The Road Map will help you think about each important person in your legacy and what they might need most from you.

THE FAMILY LEGACY ROAD MAP EXERCISE

Let's dive into the Road Map exercise itself. This is where you'll begin to see your legacy take shape in a tangible way.

Step-by-Step Guidance

Find a quiet space where you can reflect without interruption. Have your Road Map worksheet ready (you'll find the link at the end of this chapter), along with a pen and perhaps a cup of tea or coffee. This should be a reflective, even enjoyable process, not a rushed chore.

Step 1: Identify Who Matters Most

Begin by listing the people you care most about when thinking about your legacy. These might include:

- Your spouse or partner
- Your children and their spouses
- Your grandchildren
- Other family members who are important to you
- Close friends who are like family
- Future generations not yet born

Don't worry about being exhaustive. Focus on those who are most important to you right now. You can always add others later.

Step 2: Define What Success Looks Like

Write down what you want from your estate and legacy plan; what success will look like for you. Be honest about your hopes and desires. What do you want your loved ones to experience, understand, or be able to do because of what you leave behind?

I used the analogy of a relay race in earlier chapters. Perhaps success for you means passing the baton to the next generation so they can run their own race well. Or maybe success means ensuring your loved ones know unequivocally that they are loved, they matter, and they have a unique purpose.

Step 3: Understand Your "Why"

Now, dive deeper into why passing on both your financial capital and your human capital (wisdom, life stories, and love) is important to you.

For your financial capital, consider:

- Why do you want your loved ones to receive these resources?

- What do you hope they'll do (or not do) with them?
- How might these resources support their journey?

For your human capital, reflect on:

- What wisdom has served you well that might benefit them?
- Which stories from your life might help them understand themselves better?
- How might your expressed love sustain them during difficult times?

Step 4: Identify What Was Missing in Your Own Inheritance

This is a powerful question: What is one thing you didn't inherit, but wish you had? Often, what we most want to pass on is what we ourselves missed receiving.

Perhaps, like my client Greg, it was a religious foundation or spiritual guidance that took him decades to find on his own. Maybe it was financial literacy, emotional openness, or simply stories about your ancestors that would have helped you understand your family patterns. Maybe it was the ability to talk calmly through conflicts with loved ones rather than sweeping things under the carpet or exploding.

Identifying this missing piece can become a cornerstone of your legacy plan, showing you what you most want to leave for your loved ones.

Step 5: Share Key Moments

List three of the best moments or experiences in your life that might help your loved ones understand who you are. These don't have to be grand achievements—they might be simple moments of joy, connection, or clarity that shaped you.

Similarly, identify three of the most challenging experiences that have formed you. Remember, an authentic legacy includes both triumphs and struggles. Your descendants need to see that you navigated difficulties and emerged with wisdom to share.

Step 6: Envision the Emotional Impact

How will you feel when you have tangible ways to pass your TrueWealth to your loved ones? Imagining this emotional payoff can be a powerful motivator as you continue your legacy journey.

Will you feel relief? Peace? Joy? A sense of purpose or completion? There's no wrong answer here.

Step 7: Choose Your Legacy Tools

Finally, review the list of potential legacy tools to gift your family and rank your top 3-5 choices. These might include:

- Personal (or Couples') Legacy Statement
- Book of Wisdom
- Family Legacy Letter
- Individual Legacy Letters
- Recording of Guided Conversations
- Video and/or Audio Series
- Book containing your hard-won life lessons
- Special Occasion Letters
- Other legacy options

Don't worry about committing to these tools permanently. This is just a starting point to help you begin thinking concretely about how you'll express your legacy.

Examples from Real Families

Let me share how a few different families completed their Road Maps to illustrate the diversity of approaches.

The Johnsons: Focusing on Future Generations

Robert and Patricia Johnson, both in their late seventies, had three adult children and eight grandchildren ranging from 2 to 16 years old. When they completed their Road Map, they realized that while their adult children knew their stories well, their grandchildren and future great-grandchildren might miss out on knowing them personally.

Their top priority became creating video recordings of themselves sharing family stories and the values behind their family traditions. They also created a series of letters for each grandchild to open at significant life milestones—high school graduation, marriage, the birth of their first child.

"We may not be there physically for some of these moments," Patricia said, "but we can still be present through our words and wisdom."

Maria: Healing Family Wounds

Maria, a widow in her sixties, had a strained relationship with her oldest daughter following a difficult divorce years earlier. When completing her Road Map, she identified "healing family relationships" as her top priority.

She chose to write individual legacy letters to each of her three children, acknowledging the unique gifts she saw in each of them and expressing her hopes for their futures. For her oldest daughter, she included a heartfelt apology for the pain the family breakdown had caused and shared lessons she'd learned through that difficult time.

"I can't change the past," Maria told me, "but I can be honest about it and show her how it shaped me—and how I hope it might eventually shape her in positive ways too."

The Wilsons: Preserving Practical Wisdom

James and Eleanor Wilson were both first-generation college graduates who had built successful careers in medicine and education. Their Road Map revealed a strong desire to pass on practical wisdom about financial management, career development, and education—areas where they had no guidance from their own parents.

They created a Book of Wisdom with lessons on money management, educational choices, career planning, conflict resolution, and marriage advice. Each lesson included a personal story illustrating the lesson they'd learned, often the hard way.

"We don't want to tell our kids and grandkids what to do," James explained, "but we want them to have a reference point when facing major life decisions or challenges. They can take what serves them and leave the rest."

How a Simple Map Exercise Transforms How You View Your Legacy

Completing the Family Legacy Road Map often creates what I call the "constellation effect." Just as ancient peoples looked up at random stars and began to see patterns—bears, hunters, scorpions—the Road Map helps you connect seemingly disparate aspects of your life into meaningful patterns.

This shift in perspective is powerful. It transforms legacy planning from an overwhelming task into an inspiring journey of self-discovery and generosity. The Road Map doesn't just help you organize what you want to share, it helps you understand the meaning behind what you've lived.

COMMON ROADBLOCKS AND HOW TO OVERCOME THEM

As with any meaningful endeavor, you may encounter obstacles on your legacy journey. Let's address some common roadblocks and how to move past them.

Resistance from Family Members

"My kids aren't interested in this stuff. They roll their eyes whenever I start talking about the old days."

I hear this regularly, especially from clients with teenage or young adult children who are appropriately focused on their own lives and futures. If this is your situation, remember two things:

First, what doesn't interest your children now will become precious to them later. Many people don't develop curiosity about their family history until they reach middle age or have children of their own.

Second, there are ways to make your legacy more engaging. Consider using formats that appeal to different learning styles—videos for visual learners, recordings for auditory learners, written letters for readers. Breaking your life story and wisdom up into shorter, more engaging segments can help others engage without becoming overwhelmed.

Richard, in his seventies, found that his tech-savvy grandchildren were much more interested in his World War II stories when he recorded them as short video clips that could be accessed by scanning QR codes in a physical photo album.

Finding Time in Busy Schedules

"I know this is important, but where do I find the time?"

In our fast-paced world, finding time for legacy work can be challenging. The key is to start small and integrate it into your existing routine.

- Set aside just 15-30 minutes each week to work on one question from the Road Map.
- Use voice-to-text technology to record thoughts while driving or walking.
- Replace some social media scrolling time with legacy reflection.

- Schedule a "legacy date" with yourself once a month.

Remember, your legacy journey is a marathon, not a sprint. Consistent small steps will take you farther than sporadic major efforts.

Dealing with Difficult Family Dynamics

"How do I include honest stories when some of them might hurt family members?"

This is perhaps the most delicate roadblock. You want your legacy to be authentic, but you don't want it to cause pain.

As we discussed in Chapter 8, there's a middle ground between toxic positivity (pretending everything was perfect) and vomiting unnecessarily detailed accounts of family struggles without processing them yourself. Your legacy should be truthful but also compassionate.

Consider these approaches:

- Focus on the lessons learned rather than assigning blame
- Acknowledge difficulties without excessive detail
- Emphasize forgiveness and growth
- When discussing challenging people or situations, balance honest acknowledgment with empathy

Caroline, whose father struggled with alcoholism, found a way to include this reality in her legacy without diminishing him: "My father faced demons that began long before I was born, and he fell into the pattern that he watched his father struggle with: using alcohol to numb the pain and fear. His struggle taught me about compassion, forgiveness, and the importance of seeking help when needed. Despite his challenges, he showed love in the ways he could, and those moments shaped me too."

YOUR TURN: COMPLETING YOUR FAMILY LEGACY ROAD MAP

Now it's time to complete your own Family Legacy Road Map. Find the link to the worksheet at the end of this chapter.

Give yourself the gift of uninterrupted time to reflect on these questions. There are no right or wrong answers, only your truth, your wisdom, and your love waiting to be discovered and shared.

As you work through the Road Map, remember that this is just the beginning of your journey. Like any good map, it shows you the terrain ahead and helps you chart your course, but the real adventure lies in the journey itself.

When you've completed your Road Map, take a moment to celebrate this first step. You've already done something significant for your loved ones and for yourself. You've begun the process of transforming your life experiences into a legacy that will outlive you and continue to nurture generations to come.

In the next chapter, we'll dive deeper into identifying and articulating your core values—the fundamental principles that have guided your life and that you hope will guide your loved ones as well.

REFLECTION QUESTIONS

1. What surprised you most as you completed your Family Legacy Road Map?
2. Which areas of your legacy feel most developed already, and which need the most attention?
3. How did it feel to identify one thing you didn't inherit but wish you had? How might providing this for your loved ones heal something in your own story?
4. If you could accomplish only one thing with your TrueWealth legacy, what would it be?

ACTION STEPS

1. Complete your Family Legacy Road Map worksheet.
2. Share your "why" (why passing on your wisdom, life stories, and love matters to you) with at least one loved one.
3. Choose one legacy tool from your top 3-5 preferences and schedule time in the next week to begin working on it.
4. Create a simple calendar or timeline for your legacy journey, scheduling regular time for reflection and creation.

THE FAMILY LEGACY ROAD MAP WORKSHEET

Download your TrueWealth Family Legacy^{SM} Road Map today at

TrueWealthFamily.com/Roadmap

CHAPTER 10

CAPTURING YOUR LIFE'S MOST IMPORTANT STORIES

"Mom, tell me again about the time you got lost in New York City."

Every family has them, those stories that get told and retold at holiday gatherings, around campfires, or during long car rides. The ones that make everyone lean in a little closer. The ones that make us laugh until we cry or nod in solemn understanding.

These aren't just entertaining anecdotes. They're the vessels that carry our family's wisdom through time.

When my client Eleanor's granddaughter asked for the New York story again, Eleanor thought it was just because it was exciting: a 17-year-old girl alone in a big city in the 1960s, missing her bus home, having to navigate unfamiliar subway lines with only pocket change and her wits. But years later, when that same granddaughter found herself stranded in a foreign country during a study abroad mishap, she told Eleanor, "I kept thinking about your New York story, how you stayed calm, how you problem-solved. It helped me figure out what to do."

This is the power of stories. They don't just connect us to our past—they equip us for our future.

In this chapter, we'll explore how to identify and capture your most significant life stories, the ones that contain the wisdom your loved ones will need long after you're gone. We'll walk through practical exercises to help you remember these key moments and techniques to make your stories come alive for generations to come.

WHY STORIES ARE THE VESSELS OF WISDOM

Human beings are natural storytellers. Long before written language, our ancestors gathered around fires to share tales that conveyed crucial knowledge about survival, relationships, and meaning. Our brains are wired to remember information better when it comes packaged in a narrative.

But stories do much more than just transfer information.

How Narratives Shape Identity and Resilience

I mentioned earlier in this book that researchers at Emory University found that children who know their family stories show greater emotional well-being and resilience. Specifically, they discovered that children who can answer questions about their family history, where their grandparents grew up, how their parents met, challenges the family has faced, tend to have higher self-esteem and a stronger sense of control over their lives.

Why? Because family stories help us understand that we're part of something larger than ourselves. They give us context for our own experiences. They provide a space for us to live into them. Family stories create a reality into which we can choose to live.

Michael, a military veteran in his seventies, described it beautifully: "When my grandson was being bullied at school, I told him about the time I was ostracized in boot camp. I wasn't trying to say, 'I had it worse' or 'just tough it out.' I wanted him to see that this painful moment was just one chapter in a much longer story; his story, our family's story. And that gave him perspective. It really seemed to help."

Stories don't just tell us about the past; they shape how we understand our present and approach our future.

The Power of Authentic Sharing

Many of us are tempted to sanitize our life stories, especially when sharing them with younger generations. We want to appear wise, successful, moral; the perfect ancestor handing down perfect wisdom. And we don't want to simply "dump" the harder parts of our stories on our loved ones.

But there's a profound power in authenticity.

Grace, a retired nurse in her eighties, worried about sharing the story of her divorce in her legacy materials. "It was such a failure," she told me. "Why would I want my grandchildren to know about that?"

When I asked what wisdom she had gained through that painful experience, she paused. "I learned that you can survive things you think will destroy you. I learned about forgiveness—of others and myself. I learned to rebuild."

"Don't you think that wisdom might be valuable to them someday?" I asked.

Her eyes widened. "I never thought of it that way."

The most powerful stories often come from our struggles, not our successes. By sharing authentically, not dwelling on painful details but acknowledging real challenges and how we moved through them, we give future generations permission to be human and tools for navigating their own difficulties.

Stories as Protection Against Economic and Social Volatility

We live in uncertain times. Economic systems fluctuate, technologies disrupt industries, social structures evolve. The specific challenges your descendants will face may be very different from those you encountered.

But certain wisdom transcends time and circumstance.

Stories about adaptability, perseverance, kindness, integrity, these contain wisdom that serves people regardless of whether they're navigating the Great Depression, the 2008 financial crisis, or whatever challenges lie ahead in 2050.

James, who grew up during the Depression era, told stories of neighbors helping neighbors, of creative repurposing of items, of finding joy in simple pleasures when money was scarce. "I never thought those stories mattered much," he said. "But during the 2020 pandemic, my daughter told me she kept thinking about my childhood stories. They gave her practical ideas and emotional strength during lockdown."

Your stories are a form of protection, not just financial insurance, but wisdom insurance for whatever volatile times your loved ones might face.

IDENTIFYING YOUR KEY LIFE MOMENTS

Now that we understand why stories matter so much, let's focus on identifying which of your life experiences contain the most valuable wisdom to pass on.

The Lifetime Highs and Lows Exercise

One of the most powerful exercises I use with clients is mapping the highs and lows of their lives. This isn't about creating an exhaustive chronology, it's about identifying moments of significant impact, emotion, and transformation.

Here's how to do it:

1. Find a quiet space where you can reflect without interruption.
2. Divide your life into chapters or stages. You might use decades (0-10, 11-20, etc.) or life phases (early childhood, school years, young adulthood, etc.).
3. For each stage, identify 2-3 high points—moments of joy, achievement, connection, or positive transformation.

4. Then identify 2-3 low points—moments of challenge, loss, disappointment, or struggle.
5. Map your highs and lows into a chronological life story on a large piece of paper, showing the ups and the downs visually and marking them with words to indicate what happened. Find a friend or family member to do this with and share your stories with each other. Having your life story witnessed can be a powerful experience, especially if it's the first time you've told your whole story recently. You have an opportunity to rewrite it as you tell it from a fresh perspective.
6. To go deeper, take the high and low points that made a deep impact and jot down a brief description of:
    - What happened
    - How you felt
    - What you learned

Don't worry about perfect prose or complete sentences. This is a brainstorming exercise to help surface the significant moments of your life.

When Thomas, a retired business owner, completed this exercise, he was surprised by what emerged. "I thought my biggest stories would be about business successes—landing major contracts, expanding internationally. But what came up were more personal moments: the night my father taught me to change a tire in the pouring rain, the time I had to fire my best friend, the day I realized my son was smarter than me in some important ways."

These were the moments that had shaped his character and contained the wisdom he most wanted to pass on.

Finding Patterns and Themes in Your Journey

After completing your highs and lows map, step back and look for patterns. What themes emerge? What challenges have repeatedly tested you? What strengths have consistently served you well?

Patterns reveal deeper truths about who we are and what wisdom we've accumulated.

Sophia, a community organizer in her sixties, noticed that many of her high points involved bringing people together across differences. Many of her low points involved times when she felt isolated or disconnected. "I hadn't realized how central connection has been to my life story," she said. "That's the wisdom I want to pass on: how to build bridges, how to create community, how to find strength in togetherness."

You might notice patterns around:

- Resilience and overcoming obstacles
- Relationships and connection
- Learning and growth
- Service to others
- Faith and spirituality
- Work and purpose
- Adventure and exploration

These patterns point to the core wisdom you've accumulated, wisdom that deserves to be preserved and shared.

DISCOVERING THE WISDOM YOU DIDN'T KNOW YOU HAD

Something magical happens during this process of reflection: many people discover wisdom they didn't know they possessed.

"I'm just an ordinary person," Rebecca told me when I first met her. "I haven't done anything special or extraordinary. I don't know what wisdom I could possibly share."

But as she mapped her life's highs and lows, she began to see how she had navigated significant challenges: raising three children as a single mother after her husband's early death, putting herself through nursing school in her forties, caring for her aging parents while working full-time. She had developed profound wisdom about perseverance, finding joy in difficult circumstances, and creating family bonds without a traditional family structure.

"I never saw any of that as wisdom," she said. "It was just what I had to do."

This is common. We often discount our own experiences because we've lived them day by day, choice by choice. But when we step back and see the full tapestry of our lives, the wisdom becomes visible.

Your experiences, whether dramatic or quiet, public or private, have taught you valuable lessons. Those lessons are worth sharing.

TECHNIQUES FOR EFFECTIVE STORYTELLING

Once you've identified your key life moments, the next step is crafting them into stories that will engage and impact your loved ones. Good storytelling isn't about literary talent, it's about authenticity and connection.

Moving Beyond Basic Facts to Meaning

Many people start their stories with facts: "I was born in 1955 in Cleveland, Ohio. We lived in a small house on Maple Street. I went to Roosevelt Elementary School."

These details have their place, but they don't constitute a story. A story emerges when you add meaning: what was significant, how it felt, what changed, what was learned.

Consider this richer beginning: "The small blue house on Maple Street where I grew up taught me my first lessons about community. In those days, neighbors were extensions of family. Mrs. Peterson next door checked my homework when Mom was working late. Mr. Garcia across the street taught all the neighborhood kids to change bicycle tires. That house wasn't just a place, it was where I learned that we belong to each other."

Facts tell us what happened; meaning tells us why it matters.

When capturing your stories, always ask yourself: What did this experience teach me? How did it shape me? What wisdom emerged from it?

Adding Context and Emotion

Effective stories transport listeners or readers into your experience. To do this, include:

Context: What was happening in your life, your community, or the world that makes this story understandable? What were the circumstances that led to this moment?

Sensory details: What did you see, hear, smell, taste, or touch? These details make the story vivid and help others step into your experience.

Emotions: How did you feel during this experience? How did those feelings change? Don't just name emotions ("I was scared"); describe how they felt in your body ("My heart pounded so hard I could hear it in my ears").

Thoughts: What was going through your mind? What were you believing or questioning?

Harold, a former factory worker, transformed a simple story about getting laid off into a powerful legacy piece by adding these elements:

"It was December 1982, the middle of a recession, with snow piling up outside our windows and Christmas just two weeks away. When the foreman called me into his office, I knew before he said a word. Twenty-two years at that plant, and it came down to a pink slip and a weak handshake. Walking to my car, my lunch pail empty but feeling heavier than ever, I felt shame burning my face despite the cold. What kind of man can't provide for his family at Christmas? Those first few hours, driving around instead of going home, watching families shopping for presents I couldn't afford, were some of the darkest of my life.

But by the time I pulled into our driveway, something had shifted. I remembered my father losing the farm during the Depression, how he'd gathered us children and said, 'We lost the land, but we still have each other, and that makes us rich.' I decided in that moment that my children wouldn't remember this as the Christmas Dad lost his job—they'd remember it as the Christmas Dad was home to build the backyard ice rink, to serve hot chocolate after sledding, to really listen to their stories. Money was tight that year, but it became one of our most treasured family seasons. That's when I truly understood that a man's worth isn't in his paycheck."

This isn't just a story about losing a job; it's a story about redefining worth and choosing what kind of father to be during a crisis. The context, sensory details, emotions, and thoughts make it powerful.

Making Your Stories Engaging and Relevant

Even the most meaningful story falls flat if it doesn't engage its audience. Here are some tips for making your stories captivating and relevant:

Start in the middle of action: Rather than building up with background, begin at a moment of tension, decision, or discovery, then fill in necessary context.

Use dialogue: Conversations bring stories to life. You don't need to remember exact words—just capture the essence of what was said.

Connect to universal themes: While the specific circumstances of your life may be unique, the underlying human experiences—love, loss, fear, hope, belonging—are universal. Highlight these connections.

Be concise: Especially for written stories, edit for clarity and impact. Remove details that don't serve the core meaning of the story.

Consider your audience: Think about who will be receiving these stories. What might they be struggling with? What might they need to hear? What details might need explanation for younger generations?

Elizabeth, a grandmother of five, created different versions of her key stories for different age groups. For her younger grandchildren, she simplified complex concepts and focused on concrete details they could relate to. For her adult children and teenage grandchildren, she included more nuance and emotion.

"I'm not changing the truth," she explained. "I'm packaging it in ways they can access at different stages. As they grow, they can explore the more complex versions."

TOOLS FOR PRESERVATION

Once you've identified and crafted your key stories, the next question is: How will you preserve them for future generations?

Written, Audio, and Video Options

Each preservation method has unique strengths:

Written stories allow for careful crafting and revision. They can be read and reread at the recipient's pace. They have a certain permanence and formality that some find appealing. Consider:

- Handwritten letters (especially powerful as personal keepsakes)
- Typed documents (easier to produce in multiple copies)

- Printed and bound books (professional services can create beautiful keepsake books)
- Digital documents (easily shared but may require intentional preservation)

Audio recordings capture your voice—its tone, accent, and uniqueness. They convey emotion in ways written words sometimes cannot. They're also relatively easy to create. Options include:

- Simple voice memos on a smartphone
- More formal recordings using a digital recorder
- Professional recording sessions at local studios
- Guided audio journals with specific prompts

Video recordings provide the most complete sensory experience, capturing facial expressions, gestures, and surroundings. They create the strongest sense of presence for future viewers. Consider:

- Simple selfie videos on a smartphone
- Recordings made by a family member
- Professional videography sessions
- Video responses to specific questions or prompts

Many people combine methods. Martin, a retired teacher, created written versions of his key stories, then recorded himself reading them aloud, adding spontaneous additional details as they came to mind during the recording.

"The written versions let me craft the stories carefully," he explained. "The recordings capture my personality; the way I laugh at certain points, the emotion in my voice when I talk about my father. Together, they create a more complete legacy."

Technology Solutions for the Non-Technical

If you're not comfortable with technology, don't let that stop you from preserving your stories. There are many solutions:

For written stories:

- Dictate to a friend or family member who can type for you
- Use voice-to-text features on smartphones or computers
- Hire a personal historian or ghostwriter to interview you and craft your stories
- Use legacy services that provide question prompts and compile your answers

For audio and video:

- Ask a tech-savvy friend or family member to help set up simple recording sessions
- Use services like StoryWorth or StoryCorp that provide structured ways to record stories
- Hire a professional who specializes in legacy recordings
- Participate in community oral history projects that provide technical support

Margaret, who described herself as "completely hopeless with anything more complicated than a toaster," created beautiful video stories with her 12-year-old grandson's help. Every Sunday after church, they would record one story. He would set up the tablet, press record, and sometimes ask questions to help the story flow.

"It became one of our favorite activities together," she told me. "He's learning family history, and I'm creating my legacy. And there's something beautiful about the generations collaborating this way."

Ensuring Accessibility for Future Generations

Technology changes rapidly. How do you ensure your digital stories will be accessible to future generations?

Here are some best practices:

Create multiple formats: If you make video recordings, also extract the audio and create written transcripts.

Use standard file formats: For written documents, PDF is more stable than proprietary word processing formats. For audio, MP3 is widely supported. For video, MP4 is a good choice.

Store in multiple locations: Don't rely on a single storage solution. Consider:

- Cloud storage (Google Drive, Dropbox, iCloud)
- Physical storage (USB drives, external hard drives)
- Printed copies of written documents
- Physical copies of recordings (CDs, DVDs, though these are becoming less common)

Create a digital legacy plan: Leave instructions about where files are stored and how to access them. Include any necessary passwords (securely shared).

Consider professional preservation services: Companies like Legacy Box specialize in converting family stories from older formats to those designed for long-term accessibility.

Update periodically: Every 5-10 years, consider transferring important stories to current technology formats.

Robert, a tech-savvy grandfather, created a simple website for his family stories with basic HTML—a format he believes will remain readable for decades. He also printed physical copies of all written stories and stored them with his will and trust documents.

"Technology will change," he acknowledged, "but I've tried to make it as easy as possible for my stories to travel into the future."

The Future of Your Wisdom and Stories

As I write this, AI is growing in popularity and use and we're just beginning to see the possibilities it will usher into the future. My prediction is that, whether or not it feels comfortable to you today, one day in the future your descendants will not only watch the videos you've recorded but they'll be able to upload your recorded wisdom, stories, and videos into AI-powered tools and have conversations with you, asking for your advice and receiving it real-time. They will be able to tap into your wisdom and stories, and lean into your love for them, anytime and anywhere. While I'm a big believer in real relationships with real people, leaving your wisdom, stories, and love will continue to have an even greater impact in your descendants lives if these elements of the *real* you are recorded for them while you're still here and upgraded by future technology.

YOUR TURN: STARTING YOUR STORY COLLECTION

Now it's time to begin collecting your own key life stories. Here are some steps to get started:

1. **Complete the Lifetime Highs and Lows exercise**. Take your time with this—it's the foundation for all your story work.
2. **Choose one high point and one low point** that feel particularly significant. These will be your first stories to develop fully.
3. **For each chosen moment, answer these questions:**

    - What happened? (The basic facts)
    - What was happening around me? (The context)
    - What did I see, hear, feel? (Sensory details)
    - What was I thinking and feeling? (Internal experience)
    - How did this experience change me?

- What wisdom did I gain that might help my loved ones?

4. **Choose your first preservation method.** Start with whatever feels most comfortable—you can always add other formats later.
5. **Set a regular time** for story work. Even 30 minutes a week will build your collection steadily.

Remember, this is not about creating perfect, polished stories. It's about preserving the wisdom your life has given you so it can continue to serve future generations.

Your stories matter. They are uniquely yours, yet they contain universal wisdom. They are perhaps the most valuable inheritance you can leave—more precious than any material possession because they contain the essence of who you are and what you've learned on your journey.

In the next chapter, we'll explore how to identify and articulate your core values—the principles that have guided your life and that you hope will guide your loved ones as well.

REFLECTION QUESTIONS

1. What story from your life do people most often ask you to tell? What wisdom might be embedded in that story?
2. If you could ensure your descendants knew just one story from your life, which would it be and why?
3. What challenging experience have you survived that might provide guidance to future generations facing their own difficulties?
4. What patterns do you notice across your life's high points? Your low points?
5. What wisdom did you gain from your family stories? What stories do you wish your ancestors had preserved for you?

ACTION STEPS

1. Complete the Lifetime Highs and Lows exercise.
2. Select one significant life experience and develop it into a complete story using the questions provided.
3. Choose your preferred preservation method and create your first legacy story.
4. Share one story with a trusted friend or family member and ask for feedback about what wisdom they hear in it.
5. Schedule regular time for story work in your calendar.
6. Join the TrueWealth community at TrueWealthFamily.com for access to more examples and evolving technological guidance, including the use of AI in gifting your living legacy.

CHAPTER 11

EXPRESSING LOVE THAT LASTS GENERATIONS

There's a small brass box sitting on my friend Sharon's desk as I write this chapter. It's weathered and dented, small enough to fit in her outstretched hand. It belonged to her grandmother, who kept her most treasured mementos inside: a pressed flower from her wedding bouquet, a tiny silver spoon, a lock of Sharon's father's baby hair.

But the real treasure wasn't the box or even its contents. It was the letter Sharon found tucked inside after she died, yellowed with age but preserved with care. "To my dear grandchildren," it began, and what followed were three pages of love, wisdom, and hopes for our futures that Sharon's read so many times she knows them by heart.

"You are loved more than you can possibly understand until perhaps you have children of your own," she wrote. "Whatever challenges you face, whatever mistakes you make, this love remains constant. It is the truest thing I know."

The material possessions Sharon's grandmother left behind have mostly been dispersed, used up, or forgotten. But her words of love continue to anchor Sharon, especially during difficult times. They are the most valuable inheritance she could have left.

Love, approval, validation, and affirmation are some of the most powerful tools we can use to help our loved ones thrive, now and when we're gone. In this chapter, we'll explore how to create expressions of love that will outlast you and continue to nurture your loved ones for generations to come. These aren't just sentimental gestures, they're powerful tools for healing, guidance, and connection that can transform your family for generations.

WHY EXPRESSIONS OF LOVE MATTER MOST

We all hope our loved ones know how much we care about them. We demonstrate our love through our actions; showing up for important events, making sacrifices for their benefit, providing for their needs. But there's something uniquely powerful about explicit expressions of love, especially when they're preserved in a form that can be revisited again and again. And so many people fail to fully express their love that Bronnie Ware, who spent many years in palliative care, declared "I wish I'd had the courage to express my feelings" as one of the top 5 regrets of the dying.

The Power of Preserved Messages

In an earlier chapter, I shared Sarah's story—how a simple voicemail from her mom about her garden became an extraordinary treasure when her mom died unexpectedly.

While we can't predict which of our communications might be preserved, we can intentionally create messages of love designed to last. When we do, we provide our loved ones with emotional anchors they can return to throughout their lives.

Research on What Heirs Truly Value

I've previously mentioned the Allianz study on legacy planning showing that the non-financial legacy is ten times more important than the money and financial assets. Similar studies have found that what people most regret not having from deceased loved ones are:

- Written or recorded expressions of love and pride
- Life wisdom and advice for difficult situations
- Stories about family history and identity
- Explicit affirmation of their value and potential

Think about what you most wish you had from loved ones who are no longer with you. Chances are, it's not their financial assets, but rather their wisdom, stories, and explicit expressions of how they felt about you.

How Explicit Affirmation Heals Generational Wounds

Many families struggle with emotional patterns that repeat through generations; difficulty expressing emotions, criticism rather than affirmation, silence around the important things. These patterns create wounds that can last a lifetime and extend into the next generation.

Explicit expressions of love can help break these cycles.

Miguel, a client in his sixties, grew up in a family where men didn't express tender emotions. "My father was a good provider, a hard worker. I knew he loved us, but he never said it. Not once in my entire life," Miguel told me. "I promised myself I'd be different with my kids, but old patterns run deep. I was better than my dad, but not as affectionate as I wanted to be, especially with my sons."

As part of his legacy work, Miguel wrote heartfelt letters to each of his children and grandchildren, expressing the love and pride he felt but had struggled to show consistently. When he gave the letters to his adult children (rather than waiting until after his death), his oldest son broke down crying.

"Dad, I always hoped you felt this way," he said. "But part of me was never sure."

That conversation opened a new chapter in their relationship.

More importantly, Miguel's son, who had been emotionally distant with his own children, began writing them notes and explicitly telling them how much he loved them.

"It's like the dam broke," Miguel told me. "Four generations of men in our family had this unspoken rule that showing too much emotion was weakness. My letters helped break that pattern. My grandsons will grow up never doubting they are loved."

This is the healing power of explicit expressions of love. They don't just comfort the immediate recipient, they can transform family patterns for generations to come.

CREATING LEGACY LETTERS FOR LOVED ONES

One of the most powerful tools in your TrueWealth legacy is the legacy letter, sometimes called an "ethical will" or a "love letter." Unlike legal documents that transfer your possessions, these letters transfer your heart: your love, values, hopes, and wisdom.

Structure and Content Guidelines

Legacy letters are deeply personal, and there's no single "correct" format. However, after guiding hundreds of clients through this process, I've found that effective legacy letters often include certain elements. Here is the simplest template we use to get clients started at TrueWealth:

1. Affirmation of love and value

Begin by expressing your love clearly and directly. Tell your loved one what they mean to you, how they've impacted your life, and what you treasure about them as a unique individual.

2. Specific memories and qualities you appreciate

Share 2-3 specific memories that highlight qualities you admire in them. Be detailed and authentic—this helps them see themselves through your loving eyes.

3. Your hopes and dreams for their future

Express what you wish for their life—not specific achievements, but qualities like joy, purpose, love, and contentment.

4. Wisdom or guidance you want to share

Offer lessons you've learned that might serve them, presented not as commands but as loving guidance.

5. Acknowledgment of challenges or regrets

If appropriate, acknowledge difficulties in your relationship or mistakes you've made. This can be deeply healing for both of you.

6. Closing affirmation

End with another clear statement of your love and confidence in them.

To write the most impactful letter, here are a few things we recommend:

- Express your heart
- Focus on affirmation rather than criticizing or correcting (never leave criticism in writing, the damage runs deep)
- Keep it simple
- Finish … you can always add to it later!

Here's a brief example from Elizabeth to her teenage granddaughter:

My dearest Sophia,

As I write this, you're just beginning your journey into adulthood, and my heart overflows with love for you. From the day you were born—when you gripped my finger with your tiny hand and seemed to look straight into my soul with those wise eyes—you have brought immeasurable joy to my life.

I treasure how you approach life with both courage and compassion. I remember when you were nine and found that injured bird in the backyard. While other children might have been afraid or indifferent, you built it a little shelter and checked on it daily until it could fly again. That blend of tenderness and practicality is so uniquely you.

I also admire your quiet determination. When you decided to learn photography last year, you didn't just dabble—you studied techniques, practiced constantly, and gradually developed your own beautiful style. That patience and commitment will serve you well throughout your life.

My deepest hope for you is a life rich with meaningful connections and purpose. I hope you find work that engages your mind and heart, relationships that nourish your spirit, and enough challenges to keep you growing.

If I could offer any wisdom from my 78 years on this earth, it would be this: Don't rush through the seasons of your life trying to get to the "good part." Each stage has its gifts and lessons. And remember that most regrets come not from what we attempt and fail, but from what we never try at all.

I haven't always been the perfect grandmother. I've been overly cautious at times, wanting to protect you from every hurt.

Forgive me for those moments when fear overshadowed faith in your capabilities.

Know that my love for you is constant and unconditional.

Whatever paths you choose, whatever mountains or valleys lie ahead, that love remains—steady as the North Star, endless as the ocean.

With all my heart,

Grandma Elizabeth

Notice how this letter provides specific affirmation, shares values without preaching, acknowledges imperfection, and bookends everything with expressions of unconditional love.

Timing Considerations–Now vs. Later

When should you share your legacy letters? In the TrueWealth system we offer guidance and examples of why you might choose now or later to share them and may even talk through your specific situation to determine the best time to share. There are compelling reasons for both approaches.

Benefits of sharing now:

- You can witness the impact of your words
- It can deepen your current relationship
- Misunderstandings can be clarified
- It opens dialogue about important matters
- It ensures your message is received

Benefits of preserving for after your death:

- Some sentiments might be easier to express knowing they'll be read later
- The letter becomes a lasting comfort during grief
- Certain guidance may be more relevant after you're gone
- It provides an ongoing connection to you
- Your preserved words carry an extra weight when you're gone

Many clients choose to do both, writing letters to be shared now as well as letters to be opened after their death or at specific future milestones.

James, a client with terminal cancer, wrote a series of letters for his 12-year-old daughter: one to give before his death, others to be opened at significant life events: her high school and college graduations, wedding day, and the birth of her first child. Each contained memories, wisdom, and love specific to that milestone.

"I won't be there physically," he told me, "but she'll know what I would have said. She'll feel my love at those moments when she might miss me most."

Examples of Transformative Legacy Letters

Legacy letters can transform relationships and lives in surprising ways. Here are a few examples from my clients:

Healing an estrangement:

Maria had been estranged from her son for nearly a decade following his marriage to a woman she initially disapproved of. As part of her legacy work, she wrote him a letter expressing her regret, acknowledging her mistake, and affirming her unconditional love. Instead of waiting, she decided to mail it.

Two weeks later, he called. The conversation was tentative at first, but it opened a door. Three months later, she met her grandchildren for the first time.

"I thought I was writing that letter as part of my end-of-life planning," Maria told me. "Instead, it gave me a new beginning with my son."

Providing strength during difficulty:

Robert wrote letters to each of his grandchildren before his death from cancer. Years later, his grandson Michael faced his own cancer diagnosis at 29. Michael told his mother that reading and rereading his grandfather's letter helped him find courage.

"Grandpa wrote about facing his own mortality with grace," Michael said. "He told me he believed I had that same grace in me. During my darkest moments in treatment, his words helped me find it."

Clarifying values across generations:

Eleanor, concerned about family tension around money, wrote a letter explaining the values behind her estate plan instead of just leaving legal documents. She shared stories about her own financial journey, what she'd learned about the true sources of happiness, and her hopes for how her legacy would impact her family's lives.

"I wanted them to understand that my decisions weren't arbitrary or about playing favorites," she told me. "They reflected my deepest values and hopes for their futures."

Her daughter later told me that the letter completely reframed how the siblings viewed their inheritance. "Instead of focusing on who got what, we found ourselves talking about Mom's values and how we could honor them. It changed everything."

BEYOND WORDS: OTHER MEANINGFUL EXPRESSIONS

While letters are powerful tools for expressing love, they're not the only option. Different people connect with different forms of expression, and the most meaningful legacy incorporates various approaches.

Personal Artifacts with Stories Attached

Physical objects become powerful vessels of love when paired with their stories. Consider these approaches:

Annotated photographs:

Select meaningful photographs and write the stories behind them; not just the basic facts ("Christmas 1982") but the emotions, relationships, and significance depicted. These annotations transform a simple photo album into a roadmap of love and connection.

Meaningful objects with letters:

Identify objects that hold special meaning to you and write about their significance. This could be jewelry you hope to pass down, tools that represent your values or work, or everyday items that carry special memories.

Frank, a skilled woodworker, left each grandchild a handcrafted item with a letter explaining its meaning. His granddaughter received a carved jewelry box with a letter tucked inside explaining that the wood came from a tree on the family homestead and that the intricate rose pattern matched one he'd carved for his wife on their 5th anniversary.

"That box is my most treasured possession," she told me years later. "It's not just beautiful craftsmanship, it's a physical connection to my grandfather's love story and to land that's been in our family for generations."

Recipe collections with memories:

Many families pass down recipes, but they become treasures when the recipes include stories about who created them, when they were served, and what they meant to the family.

Elena compiled her family recipes into a book, adding notes about her grandmother teaching her to make tortillas, the Christmas Eve when the tamales exploded because someone forgot an important step, and how certain dishes connected to family heritage and values.

"Food was how my family showed love," she explained. "These stories make sure that love, not just the food, gets passed down."

Traditions and Rituals to Pass Down

Family traditions and rituals are expressions of love that can continue for generations, creating a sense of belonging and continuity. Consider documenting:

Holiday traditions:

Explain the meaning behind your family's holiday celebrations. What values do they reflect? How did they evolve? What do you hope future generations will experience through them?

Family rituals:

Document the regular practices that have shaped your family culture—Sunday dinners, summer camping trips, birthday ceremonies, bedtime routines. Explain their significance and the values they embody.

Milestone markers:

Share how your family acknowledges important life transitions and what these ceremonies mean. These might include religious ceremonies, cultural practices, or unique family traditions for births, coming-of-age, graduations, or marriages.

The Clark family had a tradition of planting a tree for each new family member—whether by birth, adoption, or marriage. The grandfather wrote about this tradition, explaining that it represented the family's values of growth, deep roots, and creating shelter for one another. Four generations later, that grove of trees continues to grow along with the family.

When you document traditions, include not just the "how" but also the "why", the values and meanings that make them worth continuing.

Creative Approaches for Different Personalities

Not everyone connects with written expressions in the same way. Consider these alternatives based on your loved ones' preferences and your own strengths:

For visual people:

- Create a video message sharing your love and wisdom
- Design a photo book with meaningful images and captions
- Craft visual art that represents your relationship or values

For people who value experiences:

- Create a "treasure hunt" of meaningful places with notes about their significance
- Develop a series of experiences to be shared after you're gone (funded activities that reflect your values)
- Plan a gathering or trip that celebrates your relationship

For practical people:

- Create useful guides that express your love through practical support
- Pair wisdom with tangible tools they can use
- Connect your expressions of love to real-world applications

For people who value creativity:

- Write poetry or songs that express your feelings
- Create or commission artwork that symbolizes your relationship
- Design a garden or living memorial that grows and changes

David, a musician who struggled to express emotions verbally, composed lullabies for each of his grandchildren, recording them with personal messages at the beginning and end. "These songs say what I can't otherwise put into words," he told me. "When I'm gone, they'll still be able to hear how much I love them."

The most effective expressions align with both your strengths and the recipient's way of receiving love. Think about how you most naturally express yourself and how your loved ones best receive messages of care and affection.

IMPLEMENTATION STRATEGIES

Creating expressions of love is meaningful work, but it can also be challenging—particularly for certain relationships or circumstances. Let's explore strategies for different situations.

For Close Relationships

When relationships are already strong and positive, expressions of love can build on that foundation. Consider these approaches:

Be specific and personal:

Go beyond general statements of affection to name precisely what you love and admire about this person. Specific affirmation is powerful because it shows you've been paying attention.

Include shared memories:

Reference experiences you've enjoyed together and what they've meant to you. These shared reference points strengthen your connection and preserve significant memories.

Balance past, present, and future:

Express appreciation for your history together, joy in your current relationship, and hopes for their future.

Consider a series rather than a single expression:

Instead of creating one comprehensive legacy letter, consider a series of shorter messages focused on different aspects of your relationship or addressing different topics.

Margaret created a "legacy journal" for each of her children, writing entries whenever she felt moved, sometimes a paragraph, sometimes several pages. "These aren't polished essays," she explained. "They're authentic moments of connection, captured as they happen. Together, they tell the story of my love."

For Strained or Distant Relationships

When relationships are complicated by conflict, distance, or pain, creating expressions of love requires additional thoughtfulness. Consider these approaches:

Focus on your love, not the problems:

While acknowledging difficulties may be appropriate, keep the emphasis on your care and good wishes, not on rehashing conflicts.

Acknowledge your role in difficulties:

If you contributed to the strain, a sincere apology can be healing. Focus on your actions and feelings rather than blaming.

Express understanding without assumptions:

Recognize that you may not fully understand their perspective and avoid presuming to know how they feel or what they need.

Keep it brief initially:

For very strained relationships, a short, simple expression of love without expectations may be more receivable than a lengthy outpouring.

Consider indirect delivery:

In some cases, having your expression delivered by a neutral third party or after your death may allow the recipient to receive your love without the complications of an immediate response.

Robert had a difficult relationship with his daughter following his divorce from her mother. For years, communication was minimal and strained. As part of his legacy work, he wrote her a letter acknowledging the pain of those years, taking responsibility for his part, expressing his enduring love, and affirming that her distance was a valid response to real hurt—not something she needed to apologize for.

"I didn't write expecting reconciliation," he told me. "I wrote because she deserves to know she is loved, whatever happens between us."

He decided to include the letter with his will rather than send it immediately. "This way, there's no pressure on her to respond. It's simply a gift, whenever and however she chooses to receive it."

For Future Generations Not Yet Born

Creating expressions of love for people who don't yet exist presents unique challenges but offers special opportunities. Consider these approaches:

Share your story:

Future generations will wonder who you were. Share formative experiences, values, and the context of your life to help them understand their roots.

Offer wisdom without prescription:

Share what you've learned about life, love, and happiness, but acknowledge that their world may be very different from yours. Offer principles rather than specific directions.

Express your connection across time:

Help them understand that you thought about them and loved them even before they existed. This creates a powerful sense of belonging to something larger than themselves.

Create time capsules for specific ages:

Consider creating messages to be opened when future generations reach certain ages or milestones. This allows you to address the specific challenges and joys of different life stages.

Carlos, expecting his first grandchild, created a series of video messages for potential future great-grandchildren. "I realized that my grandchildren will remember me, but their children probably won't unless I create something for them," he explained. "I want them to know their great-grandfather thought about them, prayed for them, and loved them across time."

For Healing Family Trauma Patterns

Some of the most powerful expressions of love are those that acknowledge and help heal family trauma. Consider these approaches:

Name patterns without shame:

Identify difficult patterns like addiction, neglect, or abuse that have affected your family, focusing on understanding rather than blame. This validation can be deeply healing.

Break the silence:

Many family traumas persist because they're never acknowledged. Simply naming experiences with compassion can begin the healing process.

Share your healing journey:

If you've worked to overcome family patterns, share what helped you. This offers both understanding and hope.

Express love that transcends trauma:

Affirm that your love is not contingent on perfection or pretending. This unconditional acceptance is often what wounded family members most need to hear.

Caroline, who grew up with a father who struggled with alcoholism, wrote letters to her children and grandchildren acknowledging this family pattern explicitly.

"My father was an alcoholic, as was his father before him," she wrote. "I want you to know this not to speak ill of them, but because knowledge is power. These men had good hearts and loved their families, but they carried wounds they didn't know how to heal except through numbing. If you ever find yourself turning to substances to manage pain, know that this is a family pattern you can choose to break. And know that asking for help is not weakness, it is courage and wisdom."

Her son, who had been secretly struggling with his own substance use, later told her that this letter gave him the courage to seek treatment. "Mom didn't know what I was going through, but somehow her letter spoke directly to me. It helped me understand myself and find hope that I could change our family story."

YOUR TURN: CREATING EXPRESSIONS OF LOVE

Now it's time to begin creating your own expressions of love.

Here are some steps to get started:

1. Make a list of recipients. Who are the people you want to create expressions of love for? Include both current relationships and potential future generations.
2. Consider timing for each person on your list, decide whether you'll share your expression now, later, or both. Also consider what format would be most meaningful for each relationship.
3. Start with a single expression. Choose one person from your list, perhaps someone with whom expression feels relatively comfortable, and create your first legacy letter or other expression of love.

4. Set a regular time for this work. Legacy expressions don't have to be created all at once. Schedule regular sessions to continue this work over time.
5. Consider preservation methods. How will you ensure these expressions are preserved and delivered according to your wishes? Options include:
    - Sharing directly now
    - Entrusting to your successor trustee with clear instructions
    - Using legacy services that deliver messages after your death
    - Including with your will or trust documents
    - Creating digital archives with access instructions

Remember, the goal isn't perfection, it's authentic connection. Your expressions of love don't need to be literary masterpieces to be powerful. They simply need to come from your heart and speak directly to the hearts of those you love.

Your expressions of love may well be the most valuable inheritance you leave behind—more precious than any material possession because they offer what we all most deeply need: the knowledge that we are seen, known, and loved. These messages have the power to comfort during grief, guide during confusion, affirm during doubt, and connect your loved ones to their roots for generations to come.

In our final chapter, we'll explore how to bring all the elements of your TrueWealth legacy together into a cohesive whole and ensure it reaches those for whom it's intended.

REFLECTION QUESTIONS

1. What expressions of love did you receive from parents, grandparents, or mentors that have sustained you throughout your life?
2. What do you wish someone had explicitly told you when you were younger? How might your life have been different if you'd heard those words?
3. If you were to die tomorrow, what would you most want each of your loved ones to know about how you feel about them?
4. What family patterns or traumas might be healed through your explicit expressions of love and understanding?
5. For which relationships do you find it most difficult to express love? What might help you overcome those barriers?

ACTION STEPS

1. Create a list of recipients for your legacy expressions, noting what format might be most meaningful for each.
2. Write a first draft of a legacy letter to someone with whom expression feels relatively comfortable.
3. Identify one family tradition or ritual that embodies your values and document its meaning and history.
4. Choose one personal artifact that holds significant meaning for you and write about why it matters and what values it represents.
5. Schedule regular time in your calendar for continuing this legacy work.

CONCLUSION

THE RIGHT TIME TO PASS ON YOUR TRUEWEALTH

When is the right time to pass on your human capital? Just like with estate planning, the answer is "before you need it."

On September 11, 2001, the world came crashing in for thousands of families when terrorists attacked the World Trade Center and Pentagon and unsuccessfully tried to hit another destination. A few of the precious souls who lost their lives that day were given one final, brief opportunity to communicate with their loved ones.

One of those people was former Navy pilot Brian Sweeney, on his way from Boston to Los Angeles. When he realized his plane, United Flight 175, had been hijacked, he made two phone calls. One to his parents, and the other to his beloved wife, Julie.

Julie was teaching school that fateful morning, and when she came home later that day, she discovered a voicemail from Brian. It was short, he didn't have time to think about what he was going to say, but he said what was most important. He told her how much he loved her and that he wanted her to "do good and have good times."

Julie, or Jules as he called her, kept that message, and has lived up to Brian's final wish. She volunteers at the 9/11 Memorial & Museum. She eventually remarried and has two children. She is doing good and having good times, partly inspired and partly carried by a voice message that she can play over and over and over again.

I wonder how many times she's played it.

We never know how much time we have. Tragic accidents and terminal conditions happen every day to unsuspecting people. We all know someone whose time came to an end before they expected it to.

I've had people say they would recommend this legacy cultivation process to other people, those who are older. And some who've said they will do it when their kids are grown.

I invite you to consider the possibility that if you have anyone you love, now is the best (and perhaps the only) time to do this for your family.

It's never too early to do this work! If tragedy struck and your children were still young, what would you want them to have to remember and know you through the years? What wisdom do you want to make sure they'd have to get through life without you? We don't like to think about these things, but sticking our heads in the sand doesn't keep tragedy from striking our own families.

I've witnessed too many families facing the regret of waiting too long. "If only we'd recorded Dad's stories before his dementia took hold," they tell me. "If only Mom had written down what she wanted us to know before the stroke."

These are painful words I hear almost daily. The best time to begin your TrueWealth legacy was years ago. The second-best time is today.

The cost of procrastination in this work isn't measured in dollars, it's measured in lost wisdom, forgotten stories, and unexpressed love. These are irreplaceable treasures that, once lost, cannot be recovered.

In contrast, the gift of preparation creates incredible peace. Clients tell me they sleep better knowing they've done everything possible to help their families thrive, not just financially but emotionally and spiritually as well.

WHAT TO DO NEXT

As we reach the end of our journey through this book, I hope you've come to see that the most important inheritance you can leave your loved ones isn't in your bank account or investment portfolio. Your TrueWealth—the combination of your financial capital and your human capital (your wisdom, life stories, and love)—is what will truly help your family thrive for generations to come.

The path we've explored together can be distilled into three essential elements:

First, TrueWealth requires intentionally combining your financial capital with your human capital. When money transfers without wisdom, it vanishes quickly at best. It can also do significant harm as we saw in Chapter 3. But when accompanied by your stories, wisdom, and expressions of love, it becomes a foundation for family flourishing.

Second, creating your TrueWealth legacy follows a natural progression:

- Discovery, where you uncover the treasures of your life experience
- Cultivation, where you refine those experiences into transmissible wisdom; and
- Gifting, where you share these treasures in ways that will nurture your loved ones long after you're gone.

Finally, and perhaps most crucially, this work must begin now. Each of us is a gorgeous ice sculpture, every nuance of our shape formed by the lives we've lived and by those who came before us. And we are all melting. Quickly or slowly, we don't know exactly when the heat will get turned up. The door of opportunity to share our wisdom, stories, and love is available today, but tomorrow is never guaranteed.

I've guided thousands of families through the estate planning process, and I can tell you with certainty: your loved ones need more than your money. They need YOU. The lessons you've learned, the stories that shaped you, and the love that defines you.

Your First Three Actions

To begin your TrueWealth journey today, if you haven't done them already, I recommend these three immediate steps:

1. **Complete the Family Legacy Road Map** (Chapter 9). This crucial first step will help you identify what matters most in your legacy and give you a bird's-eye view of your journey ahead. Set aside 30-60 minutes in a quiet space to complete this exercise thoughtfully.
2. **Schedule time for your first life story recording.** Choose one significant story from your Lifetime Highs and Lows exercise (Chapter 10) and commit to recording it, whether in writing, audio, or video, within the next week. Don't aim for perfection; aim for authenticity.
3. **Share one meaningful expression of love with a loved one.** Select someone important to you and create a legacy letter or other expression of love as outlined in Chapter 11. Consider sharing it now rather than waiting; you'll experience the joy of seeing its impact.

These three steps might seem simple, but they represent the beginning of something profound. Each action builds momentum toward a legacy that will nurture your family for generations.

The Personal Transformation Awaiting You.

What surprises many people about this journey is how profoundly it transforms their present lives. Legacy planning isn't just about what happens after you're gone, it's about how you live today.

As you engage in this work, you'll likely experience:

- A deeper sense of meaning and purpose in your daily life
- Greater clarity about what truly matters to you
- Stronger relationships with those you love
- The satisfaction of knowing you've done everything possible to help your loved ones thrive
- A renewed appreciation for the wisdom you've gained through your life journey

My client Robert, an 82-year-old retired business owner, expressed it beautifully: "I thought I was doing this for my children and grandchildren. But this process has given me a way to make sense of my life. I see patterns and meaning I never noticed before. I feel more alive than I have in years."

That's a recurring theme for my clients, feeling more alive once they start cultivating and passing on their TrueWealth.

This is the natural result of reflecting on your life with intention and purpose and using what you've learned and experience to help the coming generations. It's part of what Carl Jung noted, that connecting to the generations both before and after us "rescues us from isolation and restores us to wholeness."

A Closing Note from My Heart to Yours

I didn't get to inherit my mom's true wealth. But today and for a limited number of days to come we have an opportunity to do better for our loved ones. We can not only communicate in a lasting way, but if we act now, we have time to do so with intention. To think about and shape what will carry the fullness of our wealth to the people who matter most to us.

This is the wealth that money can't buy.

Some of you reading this know you need to do this for your loved ones while you're still here. You don't have to do it all today. But from my heart to yours, I hope today you will take the next step.

Cultivating your TrueWealth is a really fulfilling process, and it's surprisingly fun. But more importantly, this is the most powerful gift you can give to those you love.

Those hidden traumas our descendants will inherit through their DNA can either leave a legacy of distress or they can forge a legacy of strength and resilience that will be felt for generations to come. You have the opportunity to create more intergenerational wholeness in your family.

When your time comes and your family gets the dreaded call, what will you leave behind? What will you leave behind that they will read, over and over again? That they will listen to or watch, over and over again?

I'm excited for you to take this opportunity to cultivate and gift the human capital that will support your loved ones' wellbeing for generations to come.

HOW TO GET HELP

While this book provides a framework for creating your TrueWealth legacy, many people benefit from additional guidance and support. Here are some resources to help you on your journey:

TrueWealth Family Legacy℠ Course & Workbook

For those who want a more structured approach to creating your legacy, my comprehensive workbook provides step-by-step guidance, additional exercises, and detailed examples. The workbook expands on the concepts in this book with practical tools designed to make your legacy journey more straightforward and effective and is accompanied by on-demand videos to guide you through each exercise.

Available at
TrueWealthFamily.com/Courses

TrueWealth Family Legacy℠ Workshop

For those who want to begin your legacy journey with community support, I offer a one-day workshop where participants complete foundational TrueWealth exercises together in a supportive, guided environment. You'll discover wisdom hidden in your life experiences, identify what matters most to pass on, and create your first tangible legacy expression, all while surrounded by others on the same meaningful path. Many find that sharing their stories and insights with fellow participants provides both encouragement and accountability that accelerates their progress beyond what they could accomplish alone, leaving with both clear direction for their legacy work and meaningful connections that support their ongoing journey.

Learn more and reserve your spot at
TrueWealthFamily.com/Workshops

TrueWealth Family Legacy℠ Retreat

I periodically host an intimate retreat where a small group of legacy creators gather for three and a half transformative days. In this supportive environment, you'll be guided through each stage of the TrueWealth process, receive personalized feedback, and leave with significant portions of your legacy already completed. Many participants find that the community aspect of these workshops provides both accountability and inspiration. These retreats take place at inspiring locations, and you're encouraged to spend an extra day or two reflecting on the beautiful legacy you've created.

Learn more and reserve your seat at
TrueWealthFamily.com/Workshops

1-1 TrueWealth Family[SM] Legacy Journeys

For those who desire concierge-level guidance, my 1-1 TrueWealth Family Legacy Journey provides the highest level of support. Working directly with me, you'll receive a customized program and guidance tailored to your unique family situation and legacy goals. Together, we'll create a comprehensive TrueWealth legacy that perfectly expresses your wisdom, stories, and love. This Journey can be tailored to any individual, a couple or a family. A six-month experience is typical, although shorter experiences are available.

This premium experience includes:

- Custom exercises tailored to your family and goals
- Unlimited communication between sessions
- Professional editing and production of your legacy materials

Space is limited as I work with only a few families a year in this capacity. Learn more and schedule a discovery call at TrueWealthFamily.com/Legacy-Studio.

Free Resources

Visit TrueWealthFamily.com for free resources, including:

- My monthly TrueWealth newsletter
- Sample legacy letters
- Video tutorials on legacy creation techniques

ABOUT THE AUTHOR

Catherine Hammond is an award-winning attorney turned author and public speaker who helps people live better lives and leave better legacies. Her lifelong passion for supporting people at a deep level fuels her work, in addition to her training in law, psychology, coaching, and transformational healing.

Catherine founded Hammond Law Group in 2005, a Colorado-based estate planning and elder law firm that guides families through the maze of planning for and navigating disability and death. She is also the creator of the TrueWealth Family Legacy℠ System.

In addition to hundreds of television and radio interviews in Colorado, Chicago, Las Vegas, and Salt Lake City, Catherine has been featured nationally in People Magazine and Newsweek, and her writing has been featured in HuffPost.

Catherine's book *Hope(less): The Truth About Hope and Where to Find It* is an Amazon bestseller.

She lives in Colorado with her husband and their rescue dogs. When she's not working with clients, you'll find her hiking mountain trails, writing poetry, or recording stories for her four beloved grandchildren.

APPENDIX A

ESTATE PLANNING BASICS FOR TRUEWEALTH TRANSFER

WHAT IS ESTATE PLANNING?

The legal and financial side of estate planning is simply organizing your affairs so your wishes are followed if you die or can't make decisions for yourself. Most people think it's just about money and property, but the TrueWealth approach is different. It's about passing on everything that matters—your money AND the life lessons, values, and wisdom you've learned along the way.

Think of it this way: your estate includes two types of wealth. Your financial wealth is obvious—your house, savings, investments. But your human wealth is just as valuable—the principles you live by, the lessons you've learned from mistakes, and the values that guide your family.

Good estate planning makes sure both types of wealth reach the people you care about.

WHY YOU NEED A LEGAL PLAN (WHETHER OR NOT YOU'RE RICH)

Here's the truth: if you don't make a plan, the government will make one for you. And their plan probably won't match what you want.

Estate planning helps you:

- Decide who gets what (instead of letting a judge decide)
- Avoid family fights over money and belongings
- Make sure you get the care you want, and don't receive care that you don't want
- Keep your private business private
- Save your family time, money, and stress
- Make sure your values and life lessons don't get lost

The key is being proactive. It's much easier to prevent problems than to fix them after they happen.

THE ESSENTIAL DOCUMENTS YOU NEED

Every good estate plan has several important papers. Think of them as different tools that each do a specific job.

Your Will: The Basic Instructions

A Will is a legal document that tells everyone what you want to happen to your stuff after you die. It's like leaving detailed instructions.

What your Will does:

- Says who gets your property and money
- Names someone to be in charge of carrying out your wishes (called an executor)
- If you have young children, your will names who should take care of them (guardians)

How it works: After you die, your Will goes to court (this is called probate) and an Executor or Personal Representative is appointed. A judge makes sure it's valid, your debts get paid, and then your assets get distributed according to your instructions.

For TrueWealth: Your Will can also include a letter to your family explaining your values, sharing important life lessons, or telling stories you want remembered. This isn't legally required, but it's a powerful way to pass on your human wealth.

Trusts: The Smart Container

Think of a Revocable Living Trust like a special container that holds your stuff. You put your assets in the container, write instructions for how they should be used, and pick someone reliable to follow those instructions.

What a Living Trust does:

- Holds your money and property
- Gives detailed instructions about when and how to distribute everything
- Can work while you're alive and continue after you die
- Keeps everything private (no court involvement)

How it works: You create the Trust and move your assets into it. You can be in charge of it while you're alive and able. When you die or become unable to manage things, someone you've chosen (a successor trustee) takes over and follows your instructions, without having to go through the probate court.

Why trusts are powerful for TrueWealth:

- If done properly, you avoid the legal probate process if you become incapacitated and when you die
- You can include instructions about family values and expectations

- You can require beneficiaries to participate in family meetings or education
- You can structure distributions to encourage positive behaviors or prevent distributions before beneficiaries are financially mature
- Inheritances can be managed for children and disabled beneficiaries to provide protection
- Everything stays private, protecting your family from outside interference

Powers of Attorney: Your Backup Decision-Makers

These documents pick someone to make decisions for you if you can't make them yourself.

Financial Power of Attorney: Names someone to handle your money and business if you become unable to do so. This person can pay bills, manage investments, and make other financial decisions according to your values and wishes. NOTE: most financial institutions will only accept a POA for a limited time, often 6 months to a year, after you sign it, sending you into "living probate". This is one of the reasons we recommend Living Trusts for many clients, especially those who own real estate.

Healthcare Power of Attorney and Advance Directive: Names someone to make medical decisions for you if you can't speak for yourself. You can also write down your preferences about medical care, so your family knows what you want and don't want.

Universal HIPAA Release: Without a specific release, under the privacy provisions of HIPAA no one is entitled to speak to medical providers about your health condition, location, or care. This means that hospitals may not be willing to disclose to a spouse or a parent of an adult child whether you are in their facility and, if so, what room number, and doctors may not be willing to discuss your status or care with your loved ones.

Why these matter: Without these documents, your family might have to go to court to get permission to help you, which takes time and costs money when you need help most.

WHAT IS PROBATE AND WHY SHOULD YOU AVOID IT?

Probate is the court process that happens when someone dies. The court supervises paying debts and distributing property according to the Will (or according to state law if there's no Will).

How Probate Works

Here's what typically happens:

1. Someone files the Will with the court
2. The court appoints an executor to handle everything
3. The executor makes a list of all assets and debts
4. The executor pays the debts and taxes
5. What's left gets distributed to beneficiaries
6. The court closes the case

In Colorado, this process usually takes 9 months to 2 years, sometimes longer, depending on the state the decedent lived in, the complexity of the estate, and how well everyone gets along.

Why Probate Is a Problem

It's public: This means nosy neighbors, potential scammers, or anyone else can see exactly what you owned and who got what.

It's slow: Your family can't access most of your assets until probate is finished. This can create financial hardship right when they're grieving.

It's expensive: Court fees, attorney fees, and other costs can eat up 2-7% of your estate's gross value.

It's stressful: There are a lot of tasks and forms to be completed, and they must be done just right, at the right time. The formal legal process can also turn family disagreements into expensive court battles.

It ignores your human wealth: Probate only deals with legal and financial matters. Your values, stories, and life lessons get lost in the paperwork.

HOW TO AVOID PROBATE

The good news is that you can set things up so most or all of your assets skip probate entirely.

Recommended Strategy: Use a Living Trust

This is the most complete solution, especially if you have any real estate. Here's how it works:

1. **Create the trust:** You work with an attorney to create a trust document with your instructions
2. **Fund the trust:** You change the ownership of your assets from your name to the trust's name (you still control everything)
3. **Live normally:** Nothing changes day-to-day because you're the trustee
4. **Smooth transition:** When you die, your successor trustee immediately takes over and distributes assets according to your instructions, no court needed

Example: Instead of owning your house in your name, the "Smith Family Trust" owns it. You're still in complete control, but when you die, there's no probate because the trust owns the house, not you personally.

The Pros and (Some of the Many) Cons of Using Beneficiary Designations

Many accounts let you name beneficiaries who automatically receive the money when you die.

Examples:

- Life insurance policies
- Retirement accounts (401k, IRA)
- Bank accounts with "payable on death" designations
- Investment accounts with "transfer on death" designations

The Reality: While many of your assets may avoid the probate process when you name beneficiaries, there are a number of drawbacks to relying on these POD or TOD designations (this is not a comprehensive list):

- Beneficiary designations don't come into play until you die, therefore if you become incapacitated you may still go through "living probate", which is an expensive, intrusive process that puts the judge in charge of your assets even if you have a healthy spouse or other loved one who can manage your assets just fine
- Real estate still triggers the full probate process, and while some states allow you to use a "beneficiary deed" which has multiple drawbacks including that it likely disqualifies you from Medicaid benefits and it does not provide any of the protections for your beneficiaries listed below
- Your beneficiaries are not protected against losing their inheritance in a future divorce
- Beneficiaries currently on need-based government benefits will lose those benefits

- Beneficiaries will receive their inheritance in one lump sum, whether they are ready to manage it or not
- Children will receive their inheritance at age 18 or 21 depending on state law (when most young adults don't yet have the financial skills and maturity), and until that time the judge will determine how it is invested and spent
- You need to maintain beneficiary designations across all your assets, so if you have a life change you need to remember to review and/or change every designation with every company

PUTTING IT ALL TOGETHER: YOUR TRUEWEALTH ESTATE PLAN

An effective estate plan combines several strategies and gets updated regularly. Here's what a complete approach looks like for most of our clients:

The Foundation Documents

- A Pour-Over Will (as backup for anything not in your trust)
- A Revocable Living Trust for most of your assets
- Financial and healthcare powers of attorney
- A Universal HIPAA Release
- Various other supporting documents

The Probate Avoidance Strategy

- Fund your trust properly by transferring assets into it
- Keep beneficiary designations current
- Review and update everything regularly

The Human Pieces of Your Estate Plan

- Hold a family meeting to ensure your loved ones understand your plan and know what to expect
- Consider requiring family meetings or education as part of inheritance
- Write a Letter of Intent to your Successor Trustee explaining your wishes and specific instructions for using their discretion
- Share the reasons behind your financial decisions

KEEPING YOUR PLAN CURRENT

Estate planning isn't a one-time event. Your plan needs to grow and change with your life.

Update your plan when:

- You get married or divorced
- You have children or grandchildren
- Someone named in your documents dies or becomes unreliable, or their situation changes in a significant way
- You move to a different state
- Tax laws change significantly
- Your wealth increases substantially

Annual review: Meet with your attorney once a year to make sure everything still makes sense. Think of it like an annual check-up for your estate plan. You pop the hood on your car periodically, it's even more important to "pop the hood" on the plan that determines how things will go for your loved ones at the most crucial time of their lives.

GETTING PROFESSIONAL HELP

Estate planning involves complex laws that vary by state. Small mistakes can create big problems for your family. Working with an experienced attorney who focuses exclusively on estate planning is essential.

What to look for:

- An attorney who only practices estate planning (not someone who does everything)
- Someone who explains things in plain English
- Someone familiar with modern probate-avoidance techniques rather than a specialty with Wills and probate
- A professional who asks about your values and family dynamics, not just your assets
- An office that offers ongoing support, updates, and education, offering a continuous relationship with you that will support you and your family through all the ups and downs of life to come; an attorney who offers an annual estate plan maintenance program is clearly committed to the long-term view of the relationship and your plan

YOUR LEGACY STARTS NOW

Remember, estate planning is really about love; love for your family and desire to protect them. It's about making sure the wealth you've built (both financial and human) continues to benefit the people you care about most.

The best estate plan is one that reflects your values, protects your family, and ensures your complete legacy lives on. By understanding these basics and working with qualified professionals, you can create a plan that truly preserves your TrueWealth for generations to come.

Don't wait. Every day without a plan is a day your family remains at risk. Start the conversation today and give yourself and your loved ones the peace of mind that comes from knowing everything is properly arranged.

ENDNOTES

1. I Believe in Me!:How Little Ideas Become Big Dreams, by Dinah E. Corona and Luisa F. Molano, Halo Publishing International.
2. The Allianz American Legacy Study, 2005, in conjunction with Age Wave and Harris Interactive.
3. Roy Williams and Vic Preisser, authors of *Preparing Heirs: Five Steps to Successful Transition of Family Wealth and Values*, and studies conducted by the *Economist* and the Massachusetts Institute of Technology.
4. Family Narratives Project, Robyn Fivush and Marshall Duke, Emory University, with faculty fellows at the Emory Center for Myth and Ritual in American Life.
5. C.G. Jung, "The Psychological Aspects of the Kore," in *Essays on a Science of Mythology* (Princeton, N.J.: Princeton University Press, Bollingen Series XXII, 1959), p. 162.
6. Mark Wolynn. (2017). *It Didn't Start with You: How Inherited Family Trauma Shapes Who We Are and How to End the Cycle*. Penguin Life.
7. Family Narratives Project, Robyn Fivush and Marshall Duke, Emory University, with faculty fellows at the Emory Center for Myth and Ritual in American Life.

8. Robert Jay Lifton. (1979). *The Broken Connection*. Simon & Schuster.
9. Bronnie Ware. (2019). *Top Five Regrets of the Dying: A Life Transformed by the Dearly Departing*. Hay House.

ACKNOWLEDGMENTS

This book is a reflection of what I've learned, and what I've learned has come through the beautiful humans I've had the privilege of learning from and serving.

My deepest gratitude to my dear husband, Brian, for your eternal love and belief in me and my work. You are an amazing partner in life, and also my thinking partner, book editor, and an intentional, loving grandparent to our precious grandchildren.

Darren Hardy, you inspired me to think bigger about how I could serve the world, see the best in me, and introduced me to the members of our Elite tribe who model deep service at a level that's rare: Adam Contos, Scott Daniel, Todd Duncan, Cody Foster, Georgia Hardy, Chris Hobart, Dave Liniger, Eric Douay, Doug, Misty Lown, David Mammano, Kevin Merrigan, Paul Niccum, Sidd Pagidipati, Brad Pedersen, Jonathan Roche, Paul Rushforth, Brian Safdari, Madison Scott, Marc Sparks, Chad Tompkins, Lynne Wallace and my wise friend Carolyn Thompson who taught me so much about living before she passed away. I'm grateful to each of you for showing up passionately, creatively, and with hearts for deep service.

To my mentors in Purposeful Planning: John A. Warnick (founder of the Purposeful Planning Institute), Thomasina Williams, David York, and Curtis Kaiser, you have helped me see how to serve families more deeply within the context of estate planning and the relationship that invites us into as trusted advisors.

To Chip Conley and your amazing team at the Modern Elder Academy, you are bringing out the wise elder in people who didn't know they had it in them, including me.

To the wise and courageous Rich Litvin, thanks for your mentorship in coaching and inspiration in bringing it into my work with families. This methodology would not be what it is without you.

Chris Joseph, I am constantly inspired by you and grateful for your wise mentorship. You have supported and inspired the development of this methodology, and your fingerprints are all over this book and my work with families. Thank you for your endless support and belief in me and the power of this process.

To those who helped mold and shape this book and my keynote on the same subject: AJ Harper, Andrea Lee, Michael and Amy Port, Brian Hastert, Russell Ewing, Mike Shreeve, and Chanelle Neilson, this book and this message would still be alone and lonely in my head without you. Your wisdom and giant hearts have watered this message and helped it become what it is today.

And to the many Hammond Law Group clients and families who've allowed me and the HLG team to support and guide you, we are in awe of how you love and protect your families and deeply grateful for your trust in us.